YOUTH STRENGTH TRAINING

Timothy K. Smith, Ed.M.

The Athletic Institute
200 Castlewood Drive
North Palm Beach, Florida 33408
U.S.A.

Illustrations by Punam Sirpal

Printed in the United States of America

Library of Congress Catalog Card Number 88-071550
ISBN 0-87670-25-3

Dedication

To my son, Drew

Table of Contents

Foreword

by Vern Seefeldt, Ph.D., Director
Institute For Study Of Youth Sports

Youth Sports: Benefits and Responsibilities for the Athlete and Coach

BENEFITS OF PARTICIPATING IN SPORTS

Sports for children have become so popular that an estimated 20 million American children between the ages of six and sixteen play one or more sports each year. This tremendous interest suggests that parents and children believe that competitive athletics contribute positively to children's development. Such a wholesale endorsement may be misleading, however, unless it is counterbalanced by the sobering statistic that approximately 70 percent of the children drop out of organized sports programs by age fifteen. Many of the children who drop out are the ones who could benefit most from organized sports if directed by competent coaches. Thus, every coach, parent and athlete should answer the questions, "What are the benefits of competitive sports for children?" and "How can I be sure that these benefits are available to all children who participate in youth sports?"

Clearly, sports can have both positive and negative effects on children, but positive results can occur only if coaches and athletes conduct themselves in responsible ways. Although many of the benefits are immediately detectable and of a short-term nature, the most sought-after and important contributions of sports to total development are those that last far beyond the athlete's playing days.

In order for the benefits of sports to be available for all children, they must be identified, valued and included in their practices and games. Following are some of the benefits that are most commonly associated with children's sports participation:

- development of various sports skills
- learning how to cooperate and compete
- developing a sense of achievement, which leads to a positive self-image
- development of an interest in and a desire to continue participation in sports during adulthood
- development of independence
- developing social skills
- learning to understand and express emotion, imagination, and appreciation for what the body can do
- developing speed, strength, endurance, coordination, flexibility, and agility
- developing leadership skills
- learning to make decisions and accept responsibilities

THE ROLE OF THE COACH IN YOUTH SPORTS

The coach of young athletes is the single most important adult in all of children's athletics. Other adults, such as officials and administrators, have important responsibilities, too, but no task is as important as that of the coach, who must guide young children physically, socially and emotionally as they grow from childhood through adolescence into adulthood.

The youth sports coach is required to play many roles. Most prominent among these are being a teacher or an instructor of skills, a friend who listens and offers advice, a substitute parent when the athlete's mother or father is not available or accessible, a medical advisor who knows when and when not to administer first aid and emergency care, a disciplinarian who rewards and corrects behavior, and a cheerleader who provides encouragement when everything goes wrong.

The age and developmental level of the athletes will determine how frequently the coach is asked to assume the various roles. Indeed, coaches may find themselves switching roles minute by minute as the fast-moving, complex nature of a contest calls for different responsibilities. The coach's responsibilities in each of the most common roles are discussed in the following section.

THE COACH AS A TEACHER

Although all of the coach's responsibilities are important, none is more important than being a good teacher. No matter how adept a coach is in other roles, these successes can not overcome the harm caused by bad teaching. What then, are the characteristics of a good teacher? Good teachers know what they are attempting to teach and are able to **select appropriate content** for the various levels of ability of their team members. Good teachers are **well organized,** both for the long-term season and in their daily practice and game plans. Good teachers are also **interested in the progress** of all their team members, including those who are inept and slow-learning. In summary, good teachers must love their athletes and their sport so much that practice sessions and games are joyful experiences for coaches and athletes.

THE COACH AS A FRIEND

Children play sports for many reasons, but one of the most frequently cited is that they like to be with friends and make new friends. Often, the most important role of the coach is just being a friend to a child who has none.

Being a friend to a friendless child often requires initiative and extra work for a coach, because such children are often unskilled and may have personality characteristics which make it difficult for other children to like them. Often the attention and affection by a coach is a sufficient stimulus for other team members to become more accepting, too. Regardless of the effort required, the coach must ensure that every child feels accepted as a member of the team.

The coach as a friend must be enthusiastic about sports and the participation of all children. Good friends are motivators who reward players with compliments and positive instruction instead of concentrating on errors. Good friends make children feel good about playing sports.

THE COACH AS A SUBSTITUTE PARENT

Nearly 50 percent of today's young athletes are likely to live in single-parent families. Whether or not coaches want the role of being a substitute parent, they are likely to acquire it. Even those children who live with both parents are apt to need the advice of their coach occasionally.

One of the most useful functions of the coach as a substitute parent is simply to listen to the child's problems. Frequently, the mere presence of an adult listener who inserts an occasional question to assist the child in clarifying the problem is all that is needed. As a coach, you must be careful not to judge the appropriateness of a parent's actions. In most instances the problems between parents and children are simply misunderstandings about children's desires and responsibilities. Such misunderstandings can usually be resolved by discussion, persuasion and compromise. However, in situations where parental actions are resulting in physical or mental abuse, the coach should contact professional counselors who are equipped to deal with such problems.

THE COACH AS MEDICAL ADVISOR

Medical problems should be left to medical personnel who are equipped to deal with them. However, as a coach you are usually the first person at the scene of a youth sports injury and therefore are obligated to provide or obtain the necessary first aid. In addition, your judgment is likely to be called upon in situations where an injury has occurred and a decision must be made about whether the athlete should return to practice or competition.

A prudent policy for you is to resist making decisions which others are more qualified to make. You should seek the advice of medical personnel when injuries occur. Encourage your athletes to report aches, pains and injuries that are likely to impede their performance. Despite the emphasis on short-term objectives, your job is to safeguard the health of the athletes so that they are able to participate fully in physical activity well beyond the childhood years.

THE COACH AS DISCIPLINARIAN

One of the most frequently cited values of youth sports is their alleged contribution to the behavior and moral development of athletes. However, there are instances in children's sports where coaches and athletes have behaved in socially unacceptable ways. Obviously, attitudes and behaviors can be affected both positively and negatively in sports.

The first step to being a good disciplinarian is to establish the rules that will govern the athletes' behavior. These rules are more likely to be accepted and followed if the athletes have a voice in identifying them. Secondly, you must administer the rules fairly to all athletes. Desirable behaviors must be reinforced and undesirable actions must be corrected.

THE COACH AS A CHEERLEADER

Young athletes are likely to make numerous mental and physical errors as they attempt to learn specific skills. For that reason, their coaches must be tolerant of mistakes and eager to applaud any actions that represent improvement in performance.

Young athletes respond well to praise that is earned and given sincerely. Conversely, they are not very tolerant of criticism, especially when it occurs in association with a coach's expectations that are beyond their capacities or abilities. You must know your athletes so well that your requests are likely to result in a high ratio of successes to failures. When you choose tasks that are challenging but are likely to be done successfully you are in a position to be a **positive coach**. Positive coaches are likely to have fewer discipline problems than coaches who expect too much and then focus on inappropriate behavior. Being a positive coach is a good way to build the self-esteem that all young athletes need in order to feel successful about their sports participation.

THE ROLE OF THE ATHLETE

A successful youth sports experience places demands on athletes as well as coaches. These responsibilities should be stated so that athletes and their parents understand what is expected of them. Some of the most important responsibilities of athletes are as follows:

- treat all teammates and opponents with respect and dignity
- obey all team and league rules
- give undivided attention to instruction of techniques, skills and drills
- always practice and play with a clear mind
- report all injuries to the coach for further medical evaluation
- discourage rule violations by teammates or opponents
- play under emotional control at all times
- avoid aggressive acts of self-destruction
- compliment good performances of teammates and opponents
- return to play only when an injury is completely rehabilitated

Summary

Youth sports are designed to provide benefits to both athletes and coaches. However, these benefits cannot be obtained in the absence of clearly defined responsibilities. When both coaches and athletes accept and carry out the responsibilities defined in this introduction to Youth Strength Training then the benefits of youth sports participation are likely to be realized.

References

Martens, R. and Seefeldt, V. (1979). *Guidelines for Children's Sports*. Washington, DC: AAHPERD Publications.

Gould, D. (1986). Your Role as a Youth Sports Coach. In V. Seefeldt (Ed.) *Handbook for Youth Sports Coaches*, Chapter 2, p. 17–32, Reston, VA; National Association for Sport and Physical Education.

Introduction

My parents bought me my first set of weights for Christmas when I was in sixth grade. I must have been around 11 at the time. The set weighed 110 lbs., which was more than I did!

I still use the bar and plates from that set, only now I combine them with other equipment I have collected over the years. Strength training was an important part of my athletic life back then and remains an important part of my personal fitness program today, 24 years later. The many benefits I received from strength training have been rewarding and will last a lifetime. You can experience many of these same benefits if you follow the principles outlined in this book.

In many ways, training for strength is like life. You get out of it what you put into it. To be successful you must set goals for yourself. If your expectations are realistic and attainable, and you work toward them in a consistent and logical fashion, they will become a reality.

My goal in this book is to provide a guide specifically designed to help a young person become stronger and healthier through safe strength training. As an outgrowth of strength training, you most likely will find that your athletic ability in other sport areas increases as well. If nothing else, strength training hopefully will help you enjoy participating in yet another physical activity.

As with any new activity, you probably have a number of questions. Questions like: Is strength training safe for someone as young as I am? How can I measure my strength levels at home? What exercises should I do? These are all common questions. In this book I have tried to answer such questions as they affect you, the young athlete. I would answer some of them differently for college or professional athletes, but their bodies are mature and much different from yours. As you read this book please keep in mind that you are young; your body is still growing. Be patient and consistent with your training. In time your strength levels will increase relative to your age and size.

The following three guidelines will help you achieve the greatest amount of success from this book:

Guideline # 1

Realize that you are an individual. You are unique; different from everyone else. This is good, as it allows your strength training to be very personal. Being an individual can sometimes be frustrating, however, especially when your friends or classmates are larger and stronger, even though you are training as hard as you can.

Accept the fact that you are at an age of rapid and somewhat unpredictable change. Focus only on improving yourself and do not worry about competing with others. There will be plenty of opportunity for that later in life. **Strive to better yourself, becoming the best individual you can for your own satisfaction.**

Guideline # 2

Accept the fact that your body will be undergoing physical changes until you are about 18–21 years old, if you are male, several years sooner if you are female. These changes will have an effect on your appearance, your coordination and your health. There will be times when you experience rapid gains in strength and there will be times when you struggle. **Do not give up!** Continue on your program, following the principles outlined in this book. These principles have helped many athletes become stronger and better at their sport. In time, they will help you as well if you are faithful with your training.

Guideline # 3

Concentrate on proper training techniques when you exercise. **Stress quality in your exercise movements rather than the quantity of weight you lift.** This not only will prove to be safer, it will produce better results as well. In time, you will gain muscular strength, improve your overall fitness levels, and become a better athletic performer. The results will please you!

Strength training is safe for almost everyone. If you or your parents have any concerns about someone your age starting a strength-training program, read chapter 1 and then talk with your doctor. Depending on your health and physical maturity, you may need to modify the programs suggested in chapters 5, 6 and 9.

I wish you good fortune with your training. You are about to enter into a wonderful world of self discovery, learning more about your body, yourself, and life. You have everything to gain, so have fun.

Tim Smith
East Hampton, NY

I. Strength Training and The Young Athlete

When the topic of strength training for the young athlete arises, two questions are often asked by parents, coaches and even young athletes themselves: Is strength training beneficial to the young athlete? What are the risks involved?

Let's start this chapter by addressing the first question. Is strength training beneficial to the young athlete?

Without a doubt, yes. As a young athlete you can derive a number of benefits from a safely designed and administered strength training program.

Benefits

STRENGTH GAINS

Perhaps the most important concern is whether or not an athlete who has not reached puberty can experience strength changes. A number of scientific studies have clearly shown that both males and females who are not fully grown do increase their strength from participation in strength-training programs. While few changes in muscular size or body weight are experienced, favorable changes in muscular strength do occur.

PROTECTION AGAINST INJURY

Studies also have shown that a preventative program of strengthening muscles and other tissues can decrease the rate and severity of certain common sport injuries. Since young athletes do experience strength gains, it is logical that they would experience these other benefits much as older athletes would. In addition, it has been clearly shown that well-conditioned athletes recover from injuries quicker than non-conditioned athletes.

SELF IMAGE

Psychological as well as physical benefits can result from strength training. Improved self-image, self-worth and physical appearance are three of the more common benefits.

IMPROVED MOTOR PERFORMANCE

Many European countries have had their young athletes participate in strength training for years along with their respective sports. The reason is clear: Strength training improves athletic performance. In the U.S., we have found similar changes with young athletes. You should feel confident that you can make similar improvements in athletic performance as well.

Risks

In the face of all the benefits, there are scattered reports of injuries suffered by young athletes in strength training. If these reports are to be fairly evaluated they must be compared to similar injuries which occur in well-accepted sports such as basketball, track, and baseball.

ACUTE MUSCULOSKELETAL INJURIES

An acute injury results from one particular incident. In strength training, acute injuries most often occur during poorly executed overhead weight lifting movements. They are usually fractures. The largest concern to the young athlete is for the protection of the bone surrounding the growth plates, which is prone to injury since it is not yet mature. There are no reports of injury to the growth plates resulting from strength training alone, however, except with isolated accidents which can occur in most any sports or physical activities.

CHRONIC MUSCULOSKELETAL INJURIES

Chronic injuries are caused by repetitious stress. The most common chronic injuries are stress fractures, sprains and cartilage damage in the knees and elbows. The majority of these injuries are considered to be "overuse injuries" and are not unique to strength training. They also occur in other activities such as running and soccer. In fact, the way to prevent them is through increased strength and flexibility training, being careful to use proper training techniques and form.

Summary

It is reasonable for young athletes to strength train if they show such a desire. Since even young children have increased their strength levels, such a program can start at any age, but you should consider several factors.

Prior to beginning a program you should undergo a physical examination by a physician knowledgeable in sports medicine.

Young athletes mature differently. To strength train safely, you must have the mental maturity to follow guidance from a book such as this or from a coach. Through safe, proven training techniques, you should experience a number of benefits with little risk.

If you would like further information on the safety of strength training for young prepubescent athletes, you can write for the
Position Paper on
Prepubescent Strength Training
NATIONAL STRENGTH AND CONDITIONING ASSOCIATION
P.O. Box 81410
Lincoln, NE 68501

The American Academy of Pediatrics (AAP) also has developed a position paper on strength training and young athletes which expresses similar views.

II. Strength-Training Terms and Principles

With any aspect of life, there are certain basic principles which, when followed, will make the road to success much easier and quicker. Strength training is no different. The principles of strength training are simple and few. By understanding and using them, you will be able to get the most out of your strength training program; you will be able to reap maximum benefits for your efforts.

Overload

The most basic principle in strength training is the principle of **overload**. The overload principle simply involves making your muscles work harder than normal. When you **overload** your muscles in a regular, consistent and progressive manner, they will respond by becoming stronger. As time goes by and you continue to train, you will need to add more resistance in order to keep overloading your muscles. This progressive increase in resistance leads us to the principle of progression.

Progression

The principle of **progression** is basic to any systematic program or schedule which continues to overload your muscles. Strength-training programs usually are constructed to overload the muscles in a manner that results in noticeable strength gains every 3–4 workouts. This becomes possible through the manipulation of exercises, repetitions, sets, resistance and rest breaks.

An **exercise** can be defined as a specific movement which stimulates specific, selected muscles. Workouts should consist of exercises which stimulate all the major muscle groups.

When any exercise movement, such as a push-up, is performed from start to finish, the action is referred to as a **repetition**. Several repetitions usually are performed in succession during strength training exercises.

5

The grouping of several successive repetitions together is a **set**. During a given workout, several sets of each exercise usually are performed.

Rest breaks should be taken between sets so your muscles have time to recover before working again. Generally, a rest period of 60 seconds is sufficient time in which to recover.

There are a variety of methods for overloading muscles during a workout period. While scientists continue to research the "best" method for strength development, most agree that 3–12 repetitions will increase strength if sufficient resistances and sets are used. Using 8–12 repetitions, you can safely train for muscular strength and muscular endurance.

Table 2-1 presents a progression of repetitions and resistance which systematically overloads the muscles. Notice the increase in repetitions that took place up until week 3, day 2. These changes indicate that strength changes took place. To continue to gain strength, the trainee needed to increase the overload. This was accomplished by adding 5 lbs. to the resistance. The progression in repetitions then was started over. This process of increasing repetitions and then weight is a common and successful format for progressive overloading in strength training. It is the method I recommend for you if you are training with weights.

Table 2-1. A Training Progression Example.

	Week 1	**Week 2**
Day 1	150 lbs. x 8 reps	150 lbs. x 10 reps
Day 2	150 lbs. x 9 reps	150 lbs. x 11 reps
Day 3	150 lbs. x 9 reps	150 lbs. x 11 reps
	Week 3	**Week 4**
Day 1	150 lbs. x 12 reps	155 lbs. x 10 reps
Day 2	155 lbs. x 8 reps	155 lbs. x 10 reps
Day 3	155 lbs. x 8 reps	155 lbs. x 11 reps

Training Frequency

How often should you train for strength? This question has plagued athletes for years. Exercise should be thought of as medication. The right kind in the proper amount can be very beneficial. If you don't take enough, you can expect little change; or, if you take too much, the effects may be harmful. This is true with strength training. Research has shown that three well-structured workouts per week will produce substantial strength changes. Often, however, people tend to overtrain. They feel that if three days per week is good, then four or five days must be better. This is not true.

Your body will be put under a tremendous amount of stress when you strength train. Because of this, it is important that you give your body a chance to rest and recover between workout sessions. One logical way to do this is to schedule your workouts so you train every other day. If this is not convenient, then try a Monday—Wednesday—Friday or Tuesday—Thursday—Saturday routine. Choose a schedule which will be easy to follow and stick to it. By alternating days, you will be refreshed for the next workout, both physically and mentally.

You may hear or read of individuals who train four or six days per week. Schedules like this are more popular with competitive weight lifters and body builders. Keep in mind, however, that you are a teenager; these people are not. They are older, more physically mature and in better shape. They have been training for many more years than you have, and they too had to start off slower at the beginning of their strength-training careers. Even now, some of them overtrain.

Stay with your three-times-per-week schedule. Train hard when you do train and strive for quality in your workouts. More does not always mean better; quality produces better results!

Sets

You should perform three sets of each exercise. If exercises are performed with strict form, proper resistance, and a full movement of the muscles and joints involved, three sets will sufficiently stimulate your muscles. Be sure to take rest breaks between the sets. If you are training with a partner, one of you can rest while the other one exercises. Your rest break should last for about 60 seconds.

After performing three sets of one exercise, move on to the next exercise and repeat the process. Proceed through your workout in this manner until you have performed every exercise.

Super Sets

As you become more advanced in your training capabilities and get in better shape, you may wish to try a system of training referred to as super setting.

You must be in good shape to try this, however, or your muscles will become very tired and very sore.

When a trainee performs a super set he groups several exercises together which stimulate the same muscle group. For example, the bench press, parallel bar dip, and the dumbbell fly all stimulate the chest muscles. To perform these exercises in a super set the trainee would perform a set of bench presses, followed immediately by a set of dips, followed immediately by a set of flies, and then would take a rest break. This procedure would be repeated two more times to complete three super sets. Several of the more advanced routines presented in this book make use of super sets to stimulate your muscles.

Repetitions

The number of repetitions you perform in each set should depend on your strength training goals and the amount of weight you are handling for each exercise. A general rule is: high reps, low weight for muscular endurance; low reps, high weight for muscular strength and size.

Someone like you, still growing and maturing, should train in the range of 8–12 repetitions. Start your training with a resistance you can handle safely for 8 repetitions. Keep trying to increase your repetitions each workout until you can perform 3 sets of 12 repetitions of the exercise in one workout, then add more resistance and repeat this progressive system. Working in the range of 8–12 repetitions will develop both muscular strength and muscular endurance.

After your body has matured physically, usually by 18–21 years of age for males and a few years earlier for females, you can start to increase resistance and train with less repetitions. A more mature body will be able to tolerate heavier weights without injuring bones, tendons, ligaments and muscles. Until then, the benefits of such a program will not outweigh the risks.

Exercise Order

By structuring the order of your exercises you can increase your endurance and also reduce your chances of injury during workouts. Two simple guidelines will help you.

Alternate between pushing and pulling exercises. This will allow you to go through an entire workout without feeling extremely fatigued. It also will help reduce your chances of becoming injured because you will be able to rest, stretch and relax one muscle group while you exercise another. For example, if you perform dumbbell presses you will be working the muscles in the back of your upper arms. This is of course a pushing exercise. As your next exercise, let's say you perform a dumbbell curl, a pulling exercise. You now will be working the muscles in the front of your upper arms while resting, stretching and relaxing the muscles in the back. After you complete your curls, the muscles in the back of the arm will be more refreshed and ready to perform another pushing movement. This will reduce your chances of injury, allow you to handle more weight in the next pushing exercise and also allow you to get through the workout without becoming totally exhausted.

Secondly, exercise your larger muscle groups first and work your way to the smaller groups as the workout progresses. Your smaller muscles help you when you exercise your larger ones because the smaller muscles offer stability during the exercise. If you were to tire them early in your workout, you might then lack the support you would need to do a heavy exercise with your larger muscles. For example, you should do a bench press before a dumbbell press because the bench press incorporates the large muscles of the chest, the shoulders and the back of the upper arms. A dumbbell press exercises only the smaller muscles of the shoulder and back of the upper arms. If you reversed the order and did the dumbbell press first, you would not have enough support in your shoulder and arm muscles for bench pressing.

Finally, perform your abdominal exercises at the end of your workout. You will need abdominal strength for torso stability when you perform many of your exercises, especially those exercises in which you lift weights over your head. By waiting to exercise this muscle group until the end of your workout you will ensure adequate support of your upper torso over lower throughout the workout, and not only perform better but be less likely to become injured.

Examples of specific exercise routines are presented in chapters 5, 6 and 9.

Types of Training

There are several methods of training for strength: **isometric, isotonic, variable resistance** and **isokinetic**. Any of these methods will produce increases in strength. They all have advantages and disadvantages.

Isometric exercises are exercises that make your muscles contract (shorten) without moving the resistance. An example of an isometric exercise would be to stand in a doorway and press your arms upward against the frame. Although your muscles are contracting, the doorway will not move. (If it does, you do not need this book!)

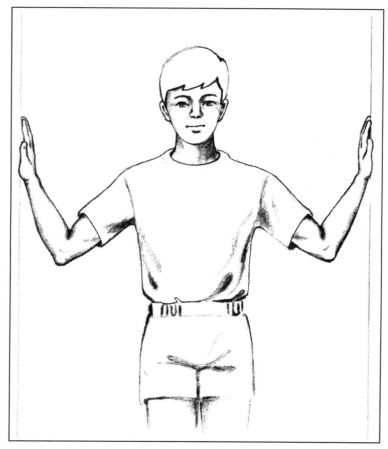

Illustration 2-1. *An example of an isometric exercise.*
Muscles strain against an immovable object.

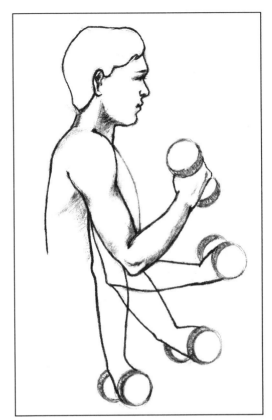

Illustration 2-2a. Example of isotonic exercise.
Muscles strain, contract and shorten. The resistance is moved through a range of motion and the weight of the resistance remains the same from start to finish.

Isotonic exercises cause your muscles to contract by moving the resistance, a barbell perhaps, through a range of motion. Push-ups, pull-ups, sit-ups, and lifting a barbell are all examples of isotonic exercises.

Variable Resistance exercise devices are designed so that the resistance varies or accommodates your changing strength potentials as you move a muscle through a range of motion. Such devices attempt to maximize the resistances you move depending upon how strong you are at each given point throughout an exercise.

Illustrations 2-2b and 2-2c. Examples of isotonic exercises.

There are several ways a resistance can be varied. A Universal Gym, for example, makes use of a lever arm to vary the resistance, creating varying amounts of tension to coincide with your movement. Perhaps Nautilus is best known for its application of this concept. Its cams vary the tension on the pulley system to provide more resistance when you are in a mechanically stronger position. Resistance can also be varied by hydraulic systems. Hydra-Gym's equipment does this. Its equipment varies resistance according to the speed at which you move.

These products represent much of the resistance equipment available today.

Isokinetic machines use variable resistance but are speed governed as well. This means that not only are your muscles maximally overloaded, but the speed at which you contract your muscles is monitored and controlled. These types of machines are rather expensive and often are found in sports medicine or rehabilitation clinics.

For people your age, training with isotonic equipment (weight training machines, barbells, dumbbells and free exercises like push-ups, pull-ups, etc.) makes the most sense because the athletic and recreational exercises you become involved in are isotonic movements. Since training is very specific to your muscular and nervous system development, it is logical to train muscles and nerves the way they will be used.

Summary

The following guidelines and principles will help you to train safely and successfully until your body fully matures. They will ensure that you experience maximum benefits with minimum risk.
— Overload your muscles sufficiently to stimulate improvements in strength (8–12 repetitions).
— Train three times per week.
— Perform three sets of each exercise.
— Perform 8–12 repetitions in each set.
— Perform exercises which stimulate all your major muscle groups.
— Structure your exercises so you work the larger muscle groups first, then train the smaller groups.
— Alternate between pushing and pulling exercises.
— Perform all of your abdominal exercises at the end of your workout.
— Train isotonically, following the progressive routines outlined in chapters 5, 6 and 9.
— Perform each exercise movement strictly, moving slowly, under control and using proper form. Do not sacrifice proper technique for heavy weights. Slow movement will stimulate your muscles as they shorten in a **concentric contraction**. It also will stimulate your muscles as they lengthen during an **eccentric contraction**. Remember, quality not quantity.
— Enjoy yourself! Be patient and consistent in your training habits.

III. Workout Considerations

Certain considerations should be taken into account before you start training. For example, where are you going to train? Will the area be safe? Will it adequately meet your needs? Are you going to use spotters or a training partner? How should you dress for maximum benefits and safety? What will you do if there is an accident? How and why should you warm up before you train? All of these questions need to be answered prior to training so that your training sessions will be safe and productive. This chapter addresses these considerations.

Selecting a Training Area

A good training area is clean, provides adequate space for your equipment, and is free of objects (tables, dressers, lawn mowers, etc.) which might get in your way if you lose your balance or drop a weight. Often when people train at home they select an area such as the basement, garage or even bedroom to store and use their weights. This could be quite dangerous if time is not taken to clear the area adequately. Plan ahead and select an area which is clean, open and well ventilated so you do not become overly hot or cold.

Training Partners and Spotters

It is always best to train with a friend or several friends. Having other people to train with on a regular basis will be motivating for you. They can offer you encouragement, and workouts will become a little more competitive because you will always want to do your best. Your training partner also can serve as a spotter, which makes sense from a safety standpoint, but also will give you confidence in trying for that last, extra repetition.

Your training partner also can serve as a coach for you by watching your lifting form and helping you maintain quality in your workouts. You can coach your partner too, and this will help you learn and get the proper amount of rest between sets.

Equipment Selection

Training on equipment that is sturdy, well built and well maintained is critical for ensuring your safety. The equipment pictured in chapter 6 of this book is equipment common to many junior and senior high schools. Your school may not be so fortunate, or you may wish to train at home, in which case you will need to provide your own equipment. Barbells and dumbbells will allow you to perform a number of the exercises presented in this book. You should also have a bench with racks for bench pressing and seated exercises. A squat rack and preacher bench would be advantageous but are not absoutely necessary for your training. If a particular sport program suggests such a piece of equipment and it is unavailable at your training site, simply substitute another exercise for the same muscle group.

Good training equipment is easy to find. Most sporting goods stores carry a wide variety of strength-training equipment and accessories that are rather inexpensive to purchase and will last a lifetime. As I mentioned in the introduction, I still have and use equipment which was given to me 24 years ago.

I do not recommend that you build your own bench or squat rack. Makeshift equipment does not hold up to repeated stresses as well as manufactured devices and can break without much warning. Good equipment will allow you to train properly and with confidence.

Proper Dress

When you dress for a workout, select an outfit which will allow you to freely perform your training movements. Tight, restrictive clothing will hinder quality movements. You also should select clothing which will prevent your muscles from cooling off between exercises. This may mean wearing a sweatsuit in the winter months that can be peeled off during the workout as needed, or wearing shorts and a T-shirt if your training area is heated.

Weight-lifting shoes, wide-soled sneakers with heel lifts, or workboots, which offer good ankle support should be worn during training. This will protect your feet from an accidentally dropped weight and help you maintain your balance. Weight-lifting shoes and workboots will raise your heels slightly. This slight lift enhances balance, helping you maintain proper lifting form. You should avoid wearing a flat-soled sneaker without a lift or going barefoot. Both mistakes are commonly made by beginners.

Establishing an Emergency Plan

It is sensible to have an emergency plan in case something unexpected happens to you or your training partner. Everyone who trains with you should know where the nearest phone is located. They should also know who to call in an emergency, what the phone number is, and how to give directions to your training site from the nearest major road. It would be a good idea to write this information down and post it in a highly visible place.

Warming Up

Before each workout session spend 10–15 minutes warming up your muscles and joints. A warm-up session will increase the circulation to your muscles and elevate the temperature within them. This change in your body will allow you to get more out of your training session and also reduce the possibility of experiencing sore or strained muscles.

To warm up, perform about 5 minutes of a rhythmic activity which incorporates all of your major joints and muscle groups. Activities such as skipping rope or easy jogging are perfect warm up exercises. Follow these activities with a complete stretching and flexibility program such as the one outlined in this chapter. By becoming flexible you will be able to get a greater stretch with your muscles and therefore increase your potential for strength because you will become mechanically more efficient. Flexible muscles are also less likely to become injured.

Stretching Exercises

The following stretching exercises are designed to loosen your muscles and joints starting with your upper body and progressing down through your legs. By performing your flexibility exercises after a brief warm-up, your muscles will be more receptive to stretching; they will be warmer and have an increased supply of blood flowing through them. It also would be a good idea to stretch again at the completion of your entire workout.

Use the following guidelines to help yourself achieve full benefit from each of the described exercises.
— Breathe freely as you stretch.
— Relax as you stretch. Concentrate on the muscles you are stretching and feel them lengthen.

— If an exercise asks you to hold a stretch, do not bounce. Stretch your muscle to a point where you can feel the stretch, without any pain, and merely hold that position for 15–30 seconds.
— If an exercise asks you to perform movements, perform them slowly, rhythmically and under total control. You may wish to pause at each end of the stretching movement.

Exercises for the Neck and Upper Body

SHOULDER ROLLS WITH STRAIGHT ARMS

Stand with your arms held out to the side as in illustration 3-1. Hold your palms down and your shoulders slightly forward. Moving slowly, bring your shoulders up and back, rotating your arms so that your palms are moved into an "up" position, finishing the movement as in illustration 3-2.
Perform 8–12 movements.

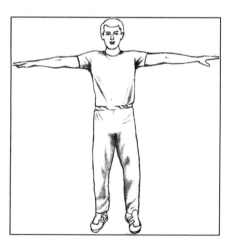
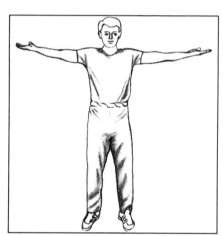

Illustration 3-1   **Illustration 3-2**

TOUCH AND PULL

Stand as in illustration 3-3 with your finger tips just touching, hands resting lightly on the back of your neck. Breathe in as you pull your shoulder blades together, drawing your elbows back (illustration 3-4). Pause, then exhale as you relax and let your elbows drift forward, returning to your starting position.

Perform 8–12 movements.

Illustration 3-3

Illustration 3-4

PRESS AND TUCK

Clasp your hands by interlocking your fingers and turn your palms outward, up toward the ceiling. Press your hands up toward the ceiling, stretching your shoulders and the muscles of your upper torso. At the same time, tighten the muscles of your abdomen and buttocks, tilting your hip region forward (illustration 3-5). This will prevent an "arching" of your low back and thus stretch the muscles in this region more safely.

Notice that your head should stay in perfect alignment with your spine, avoiding a backward tilt. You can ensure this by looking straight ahead, rather than up. Breathe continuously as you hold this position for 15–30 seconds.

Illustration 3-5

HEAD TILTS

Stand with your hands on your hips and relax the muscles of your neck and upper back. Slowly, let your head tilt to your left. Breathe freely as gravity pulls it down toward your shoulder. After 15–30 seconds, return your head to an upright position and then tilt it to the right.

Illustration 3-6

HEAD TURNS

Remain in the same stance with your hands on your hips. Turn your head to the left so that you are looking over your left shoulder (illustration 3-7). Pause, then slowly let gravity pull your chin down so that it slides across your chest toward your sternum. Continue to turn your head so that your chin slides up your right side (illustration 3-8), allowing you to eventually look over your right shoulder.
Perform 8–12 movements.

Illustration 3-7

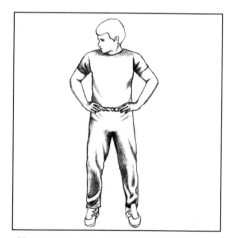

Illustration 3-8

SHOULDER SHRUGS

Relax the muscles in your neck and upper back, letting your arms hang at your sides. Slowly draw your shoulders up and back, breathing in as you do so. Use only the muscles of your upper back to perform the movement, letting your arms hang relaxed (illustration 3-9). Complete the movement by exhaling and pressing your shoulders down as you finish tracing an imaginary circle with your shoulders.

Perform 8–12 movements.

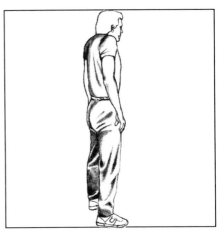

Illustration 3-9

Exercises for the Low Back and Mid-Torso Region

SIT ON HEELS

Assume the position shown in illustration 3-10. Stretch the entire spine by pressing your buttocks back and down toward your heels; and at the same time, reach forward with your hands. Be sure to keep your head in alignment with your spine.

Breathe freely as you hold this position for 15–30 seconds.

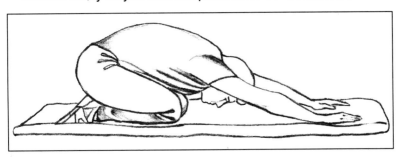

Illustration 3-10

ARCH AND TILT

This exercise has three separate and distinct positions. The first position is illustration 3-11. Balance yourself on all fours and keep your head in alignment with your spine.

Move into the second position (illustration 3-12) by arching your back and dropping your head. You will achieve a greater rounding of your back if you also slide your hands back toward your knees. Breathe freely as you hold this stretch for 15 seconds.

Move back to the starting position and then perform the "tilt" portion of this exercise by pressing your abdomen down toward the floor while tilting your buttocks up. Hold this position for 15 seconds, breathing freely as you do so.

Repeat the entire sequence 6 times.

Illustration 3-11

Illustration 3-12

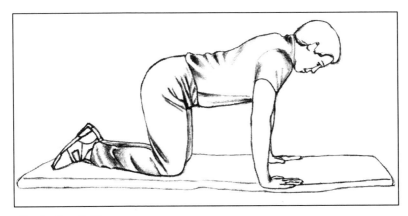

Illustration 3-13

SINGLE KNEE TUCK

Lie on your back as in illustration 3-14. Pull your left leg in toward your chest by placing your hands behind your knee. Keep your upper body relaxed and stretch the muscles of your buttock and low back. Your right leg can remain slightly bent as is comfortable. Hold this position for 15 seconds.

Switch legs and repeat.

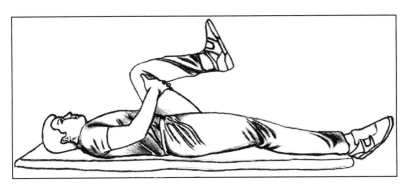

Illustration 3-14

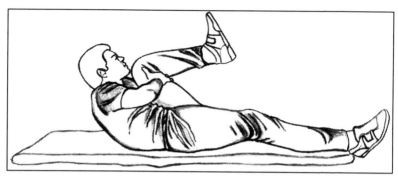

Illustration 3-15

Illustration 3-16

SINGLE KNEE TUCK AND TWIST

Start this exercise as you did the single knee tuck, using your left leg. Slowly, and with control, let your left knee and thigh drift to your right, twisting your torso as they do so. Be sure to breathe freely and keep both shoulders on the floor. Gently pull your left knee down with your right hand as in illustration 3-16, stretching the muscles in your left buttock and low back in the process. Hold this position for 15–30 seconds.

Switch legs and repeat.

DOUBLE KNEE TUCK

This exercise is identical in technique to the single knee tuck with the exception that both legs are pulled up toward the chest at the same time. Be sure to pull far enough so that the buttocks are slightly off the floor. Breathe freely and hold for 15–30 seconds.

Illustration 3-17

DOUBLE KNEE TUCK AND TWIST

Lie on your back as in illustration 3-18. Be sure that your knees are lined up over your hips. Hold your arms out to the side for balance. Slowly, with both legs together, let your knees drift to the left until they touch the floor. Control the movement with your abdominal muscles, letting your back stretch.

Illustration 3-18

Now bring your knees back up over your body and lower them down to the right side.

Repeat this left to right motion 8–12 times, breathing freely as you do so.

Illustration 3-19

Exercises for the Legs

BUTTERFLY PRESS

Sit as in illustration 3-20. Grasp both ankles with your hands and place your elbows inside your knees as shown. Sitting upright, gently press your knees to the floor with your elbows, stretching the muscles of your groin as you do so.

Be sure to keep your upper body relaxed and breathe freely. Hold the stretch for 15–30 seconds.

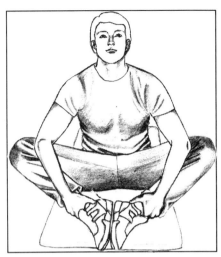

Illustration 3-20

SINGLE LEG HAMSTRING STRETCH

Move your left leg out of the butterfly press and extend it out straight in front of your body. Be sure to keep your foot in a flexed position so that your toes are pointing straight up toward the ceiling. Your right foot should remain as it was (illustration 3-21).

With both hands, reach down your leg as far as possible without bending your leg and try to reach around your left foot. Breathe freely and hold this stretch position for 15–30 seconds.

Switch legs and repeat.

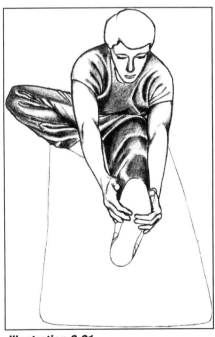

Illustration 3-21

SPLIT LEG STRETCH

Spread your legs as wide as possible, keeping your legs straight and your feet extended so that your toes point away from your body as shown in illustration 3-22.

Place your hands flat on the floor just off your hips and gently lean forward, letting gravity pull your torso down between your legs.

Breathe freely and hold this stretch for 15–30 seconds.

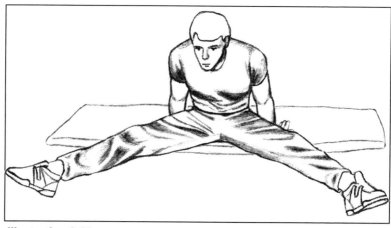

Illustration 3-22

UPPER LEG STRETCH

Stand as in illustration 3-23. Support your weight on your left leg and balance yourself with your right hand. Using your left hand, pull your right foot up behind you stretching the muscles of your thigh. Be sure to keep your body straight and your left knee in contact with your right knee so that only your thigh is being stretched. You can help to keep your back straight if you tilt your hip region forward as you did in the press and tuck stretch.

Breathe freely as you hold this stretch for 15–30 seconds.

Switch legs and repeat.

Illustration 3-23

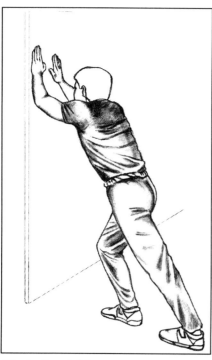

Illustration 3-24

LOWER LEG STRETCH

Lean against a wall as in illustration 3-24. Be sure that your left heel and the toes of your left foot line up so that they form a straight line, perpendicular to the wall. Gently lean forward so that you stretch the muscles in the lower portion of your left leg. You can maximize the stretch by being careful to keep your heel on the ground. Hold this position for 15–30 seconds.

Switch legs and repeat.

Summary

Take the time to prepare properly for your workouts. The extra few steps involved are well worth the effort, since you will be able to train harder and more safely, with greater motivation and confidence. The following guidelines will serve as a checklist for your preworkout preparation:

— Select a training area that is clean, neatly organized, free from potential hazards and well ventilated.
— Train with a partner. This will help to motivate you, give you confidence as your partner spots for you, and help you to maintain quality in your workouts as your partner watches and critiques your form. It also will ensure adequate rest breaks between sets.
— Use quality equipment. Do not attempt to build makeshift equipment of your own.
— Dress in exercise clothing that allows freedom in your movements, yet keeps your muscles adequately warmed. Wear shoes that provide you with good support.

— Establish an emergency plan.
— Take the time to warm up before actually training. Be sure to stretch all your major joints and muscles. Stretch by rotating joints slowly and fully. Do not bounce when you stretch your muscles; reach into a stretched position and then hold the position for 15–30 seconds.

IV. Measuring Your Physical Performance Levels

Prior to starting your strength-training program you should assess your current physical performance levels. This evaluation will help you to closely monitor increases in your athletic performance as a result of your strength training programs.

After eight weeks of training you should reevaluate performance levels; you will observe noticeable changes. By keeping track of your progress and recording these positive changes you will continue to be motivated and train with even more enthusiasm. Diagram 4-1 illustrates many of the fitness variables which contribute to optimal performance. You can readily see that a number of these parameters will be influenced by a strength-training program. The parameters underneath the dotted line are directly influenced by strength training, and it is these parameters which you should monitor most closely.

Diagram 4-1. Fitness parameters related to optimal performance.

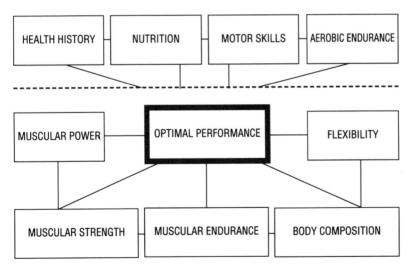

Assessment Areas

MUSCULAR STRENGTH AND ENDURANCE

The cornerstone of optimal performance is muscular strength and endurance. The measurement of this component is somewhat difficult, since test results are muscle-specific. This means that, ideally, you should test every single muscle group in your body if you want to truly assess overall strength. To do so, however, would require elaborate testing equipment and would be impractical. A number of tests have been developed which measure muscular strength and endurance in the major muscle groups like the chest, back and abdominals.

These tests are described in detail throughout this chapter. At the end of the chapter, norms are presented so that you can compare your scores to those of other individuals of your age and sex. A recording sheet has been included in the Appendix so you can monitor progress during future training. A sample of this form is presented at the end of this chapter.

PULL-UP TEST

—Dynamic muscular endurance test for latissimus dorsi and biceps.

Males should start this test by hanging from a bar as indicated in photo 4-1. Females should start in the position illustrated in photo 4-2. Your hands should be grasping the bar so that your palms are facing away from your body. Your feet should not be able to touch the floor. You may find it necessary to bend your knees to ensure this.

Males should pull themselves up so that their chins are raised higher than the level of the bar. Exhale as you pull up and inhale as you lower yourself back down to a full hanging position. Try not to "swing" or "kick" to help yourself up. Instead, just rely on the strength in your back and arms. Count the times your chin clears the bar and try to do as many as you can.

Females should perform a flexed-arm hang test rather than the pull-up test used with males. In this test you should hang in the flexed arm position for as long as possible while a partner times your hang time in seconds.

Be careful not to rest your chin on the bar, but rather keep your chin just above and off it. When you can no longer keep your chin higher than the level of the bar, the test is over.

Pull-up and flexed-arm hang norms are presented in tables 4-1 and 4-2.

Photo 4-1   **Photo 4-2**

MODIFIED SIT-UP TEST

—Dynamic muscular endurance test for abdominal muscles.

The muscles of the abdominal wall are important for posture. They also provide upper body support in daily activities and athletic events, as well as help protect the low back.

A common method of assessing their strength and endurance is the modified sit-up test for time.

Assume the position illustrated in photo 4-3. Your feet should be flat on the floor, approximately 12–18 inches from your buttocks. Fold your arms on your chest. Starting from this position you should sit up so that your elbows touch your knees as shown in photo 4-4. A partner should be holding your feet firmly against the floor. Breathe out as you sit up and then inhale as you return to the floor.

Your partner should count the number of sit-ups you can perform in 60 seconds.

Norms for the one minute sit-up test are presented in table 4-3.

Photo 4-3

Photo 4-4

MUSCULAR POWER

Muscular power measurements traditionally assess the power contained in one's lower body, specifically the hips, buttocks and muscles in the upper leg. In a true sense of the word, power is a measure of work made against time. Work simply can be defined as the application of a force (a contracting muscle) against a resistance (body weight) to move the resistance a distance. You therefore can measure the distance your body moves in a standing long jump to determine the power in your lower body. The "explosive" capabilities of these muscles are important for initiating a number of movements and skills in athletic endeavors, such as: blocking in football, jumping in basketball, sprinting in track, and a host of other activities.

STANDING LONG JUMP

—Power test for the muscles of the lower body.

Find yourself a level area on which to take this test. A concrete or other nonskid surface would be fine. Draw a line to start from and stand on the line with your toes just touching it, but not over it. Your feet should be spread so that you are comfortable; about shoulder width apart.

Prepare for your jump by bending your knees and bringing your arms back behind you (photo 4-5). When you are ready, throw your arms out in front of you, straightening your legs at the same time so you propel yourself up, out, and away from the line.

Photo 4-5   **Photo 4-6**

Measure your jump, by marking your landing spot where your body is closest to the line. Make three attempts and record your best jump.

Norms for the standing long jump are presented in table 4-4.

FLEXIBILITY

Flexibility, like muscular strength and endurance, is muscle- and joint-specific. Ideally, you should measure flexibility in each of your major joints, but again this would be quite time-consuming and expensive.

A simple test that evaluates flexibility in the legs, hips and low back is referred to as a sit-and-reach test. To perform this test you will need a yardstick or tape measure.

SIT-AND-REACH TEST

—Flexibility test for the muscles of the legs, hips and low back.

Sit on the floor so that your legs are straight with your feet pointing straight up. Your feet should be spaced 5 inches apart. Place the yardstick between your legs as illustrated in photo 4-7. The 15-inch mark should be even with your heels; the "zero" mark toward your body.

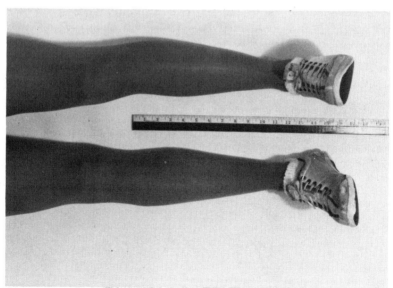

Photo 4-7

Overlap your hands as indicated in photo 4-8. With your partner holding your knees flat to the floor, stretch forward reaching as far down the yardstick as you can. Inhale before you start and exhale

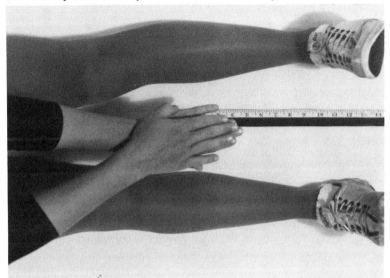

Photo 4-8

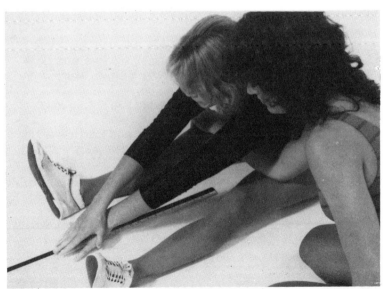

Photo 4-9

as you reach. Move slowly and under control so as not to "over stretch." You may want to stretch for several minutes prior to this test allowing yourself to warm up.

Take three trials and record your best score to the nearest centimeter. Norms for the sit-and-reach test are presented in table 4-5.

BODY COMPOSITION

By measuring your body composition you will be able to determine how your weight is distributed with respect to fat and lean tissue. This is an important concept because as you strength train your weight may change, but your composition or percentage of fat should change so that you have proportionately less fat and more lean body weight.

A body composition assessment will reveal the following five measures: total weight, percent fat, fat weight, lean body weight and ideal body weight.

Total weight—is the weight you measure when you step on a scale. This represents your overall weight, and is a combination of your fat weight and lean body weight.

Percent fat—is the percentage of your body weight that is comprised of fat tissue. You will be determining this measure through the use of a skinfold test.

Fat weight—this is the actual weight of your fat tissue and is derived by multiplying your percent body fat times your total body weight.

Lean body weight—this is the weight in your body that is fat free. It is comprised largely of muscle tissue and bone. This measure is derived by subtracting your fat weight from you total weight.

Ideal body weight—this is the amount you should weigh to help you perform optimally on the athletic field.

Perform the skinfold test described below and then use equation 4-1 and table 4-7 to help you determine your ideal body weight.

SKINFOLD TEST

—Body composition test to determine ideal body weight.

You can determine your body composition rather easily with the help of a partner and a ruler.

Let your right arm hang down at your side as illustrated in photo 4-10. Have your friend locate the midway point between your shoulder and elbow on the back of your arm, pinching a fold of skin and fat at this point. It is easiest if your friend uses his thumb and index finger to do this. The skin and fat should be pulled away from the muscle.

Using the ruler, he should measure the thickness of the skin to the nearest eighth of an inch by measuring the distance between the thumb and index finger without pressing the ruler against the skin. Several measures should be taken until two agree.

Compare your score to the scores presented on table 4-6 to determine your percent body fat. Using this number and your total weight, substitute your values into equation 4-1 to determine your fat weight, lean body weight and ideal body weight.

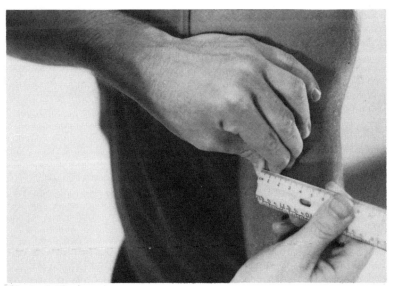

Photo 4-10

Equation 4-1. Calculation of ideal body weight based on percent body fat and present weight.

[Total Body Weight x Percent Fat] /100 = Fat Weight

[_____ x _____] /100 = _____

[(150)   x   (20)   ] /100 = (30 lbs.)

[Total Body Weight - Fat Weight] /   = Lean Body Weight

[_____ - _____] /   = _____

[(150)   -   (30)   ] /   = (120 lbs.)

[Lean Body Weight x 100] / [Ideal Percent Lean Body Weight] =

[(120) x 100] / [(90)] =

[12000] / [90] =

133.33 lbs. (Ideal Body Weight @ 10% Fat)

Ideal lean body weight percentages can be found by sport in table 4-7.

Determining Your Fitness Rating

Use form 4-1 in the Appendix to record your scores for the various fitness parameters you assessed in this chapter and to write in appropriate scores for your age. An example of how to use this form is presented on form 4-1 for a 16-year-old-male with the following scores: pull-ups 15, sit-ups 48, sit-and-reach 23 cm., standing long jump 6'10" and body composition 9% fat.

Fitness values are presented for each test item on the following pages.

Form 4-1. Recording form for fitness assessment scores.

Assessment/ Fitness Level	Pull-ups/ Flexed Arm Hand	Sit-ups	Long Jump	Sit- and- Reach	Body Composition
EXCELLENT	(15)				(9% fat)
GOOD					
AVERAGE		(48)			
BELOW AVG.			(6'10")		
LOW				(23cm.)	

Table 4-1. Pull-up norms for males.

Age Group By Year

Rating	11	12	13	14	15	16	17+
Excellent	7-20	7-15	9-24	10-20	11-25	13-25	14-32
Good	4-6	4-6	5-8	7-10	8-10	10-12	10-12
Average	2-3	2-3	3-5	5-6	6-7	7-9	8-10
Below Average	1-2	1-2	1-3	3-4	4-5	5-6	5-7
Low	0	0	1	2	3	4	5

Adapted from AAHPERD, AAHPERD Youth Fitness Manual, Revised, Washington, DC, 1966, pp. 34, 65.

Table 4-2. Flexed-arm hang scores for females (seconds).

Age Group By Year

Rating	11	12	13	14	15	16	17+
Excellent	25-79	23-64	21-80	22-60	22-74	26-74	25-76
Good	13-20	11-19	12-18	11-19	13-18	12-19	12-19
Average	8-11	6-10	7-10	7-10	8-11	7-10	8-11
Below Average	4-6	3-6	3-6	3-6	3-6	3-6	4-7
Low	0-3	0-2	0-2	0-2	0-2	0-2	0-3

Adapted from AAHPERD, AAHPERD Youth Fitness Manual, Revised, Washington, DC, 1966, pp. 27, 64.

Table 4-3. Sit-up norms.

Males

Age Group By Year

Rating	11	12	13	14	15	16	17+
Excellent	48-61	52-68	54-70	54-70	55-69	59-70	59-65
Good	41-46	45-50	46-52	48-52	48-52	50-55	51-56
Average	37-40	39-43	41-45	42-46	44-47	45-49	46-50
Below Average	31-35	33-38	36-40	38-41	39-42	39-44	40-45
Low	17-30	19-30	25-35	27-36	28-38	28-38	25-38

Adapted from AAHPERD, Lifetime Health Related Physical Fitness Test Manual, 1980, pp. 32.

Females

Age Group By Year

Rating	11	12	13	14	15	16	17+
Excellent	46-55	48-61	48-60	48-57	50-64	50-63	50-65
Good	39-44	40-45	40-46	40-45	41-47	39-49	43-47
Average	34-37	36-40	35-39	35-39	37-41	33-37	37-42
Below Average	29-33	31-35	30-34	31-34	31-35	30-32	32-36
Low	19-28	19-30	18-29	20-30	20-30	20-29	19-31

Adapted from AAHPERD, Lifetime Health Related Physical Fitness Test Manual, 1980, pp. 33.

Table 4-4. Standing long jump norms.

Males

Age Group By Year

Rating	11	12	13	14	15	16	17+
Excellent	6'0"-7'0"	6'10"-7'10"	6'11"-8'9"	7'5"-8'11"	7'9"-9'2"	8'1"-9'11"	8'3"-9'8"
Good	5'6"-5'10"	5'11"-6'9"	"6'3"-6'9"	6'9"-7'3"	7'2"-7'6"	7'6"-7'11"	7'8"-8'1"
Average	5'2"-5'6"	5'6"-5'9"	5'10"-6'1"	6'4"-6'8"	6'9"-7'1"	7'1"-7'5"	7'3"-7'7"
Below Average	4'10"-5'1"	5'1"-5'5"	5'5"-5'9"	5'9"-6'3"	6'4"-6'8"	6'7"-7'0"	6'10"-7'2"
Low	1'8"-4'8"	3'0"-5'0"	2'9"-5'3"	3'8"-5'8"	2'1"-6'3"	2'2"-6'6"	3'7"-6'8"

Adapted from AAHPERD, AAHPERD Youth Fitness Test Manual, Revised, Washington, DC, 1966, pp. 37, 65.

Females

Age Group By Year

Rating	11	12	13	14	15	16	17+
Excellent	5'10"-7'10"	6'0"-8'2"	6'0"-7'6"	6'2"-7'4"	6'3"-7'8"	6'4"-7'5"	6'4"-7'8"
Good	5'4"-5'8"	5'5"-5'9"	5'5"-5'10"	5'7"-6'0"	5'9"-6'1"	5'8"-6'2"	5'10"-6'2"
Average	4'10"-5'2"	5'0"-5'4"	5'0"-5'4"	5'3"-5'6"	5'4"-5'7"	5'4"-5'7"	5'5"-5'9"
Below Average	4'6"-4'9"	4'7"-4'11"	4'6"-5'0"	4'9"-5'1"	4'10"-5'3"	4'11"-5'3"	5'0"-5'3"
Low	2'11"-4'4"	2'11"-4'5"	2'11"-4'6"	3'0"-4'8"	2'11"-4'8"	3'2"-4'10"	3'0"-4'10"

Adapted from AAHPERD, AAHPERD Youth Fitness Test Manual, Revised, Washington, DC, 1966, pp. 36, 64

Table 4-5. Sit and reach norms (centimeters).

Males

Age Group By Year

Rating	11	12	13	14	15	16	17+
Excellent	32-38	32-52	34-41	37-43	39-47	40-45	43-48
Good	28-31	29-31	29-33	31-36	33-37	35-38	38-41
Average	25-27	26-28	26-28	28-30	30-32	30-34	34-37
Below Average	22-24	22-25	22-25	24-27	26-29	26-29	30-33
Low	12-21	13-21	12-20	15-23	13-24	11-25	15-28

Females

Age Group By Year

Rating	11	12	13	14	15	16	17+
Excellent	36-41	38-46	40-49	42-49	44-49	43-48	43-47
Good	31-34	33-36	35-38	36-40	40-43	38-42	40-42
Average	29-30	30-32	31-33	33-36	36-39	34-37	35-39
Below Average	25-28	26-29	26-30	29-32	32-34	31-33	31-34
Low	16-24	15-25	17-24	18-28	19-31	14-30	22-31

Adapted from AAHPERD, Lifetime Health Related Physical Fitness Test Manual, 1980, pp. 34, 35.

Table 4-6. Percent fat norms.

Tricep Skinfold	Percent Fat Males	Percent Fat Females
1/4 inch	7%	10%
3/8 inch	9%	13%
1/2 inch	11%	16%
5/8 inch	13%	18%
3/4 inch	15%	20%
7/8 inch	18%	23%
1 inch	20%	25%
1 1/8 inch	22%	28%
1 1/4 inch	25%	31%

Table 4-7. Ideal percentages of body fat and lean body weight for various sports.

Sport	Sex	Percent Fat (%)	Percent Lean Body Weight (%)
Baseball			
	M	11.8	88.2
Basketball			
	M	9.7	90.3
	F	23.8	76.2
Cycling			
	M	9.0	91.0
Football			
Defensive Backs		11.5	88.5
Offensive Backs		12.4	87.6
Linebackers		13.4	86.6
Off. Linemen		19.1	80.9
Def. Linemen		18.5	81.5
Gymnastics			
	M	4.6	95.4
	F	17.0	83.0
Skiing			
	M	8.0	92.0
	F	15.5	84.5
Soccer			
	M	10.0	90.0
Swimming			
	M	8.0	92.0
	F	19.0	81.0
Tennis			
	M	14.0	86.0
	F	24.0	76.0
Wrestling			
	M	6.9	93.1

*Values are approximate and have been averaged from a number of sources.

V. Strength-Training Exercises and Routines

In a strength-training program you should start slowly and then progress more vigorously as your body adapts to this new activity. This chapter outlines a strength-training program using exercises which make use of your body weight for resistance. This is a safe way to initiate strength training for several reasons:

(1) it will allow time for your body to adjust and develop a base of strength before you attempt to lift free weights (barbells and dumbbells), which may be heavy; (2) it will help you develop an awareness of your muscles as they relate to your body and body movements. This will make your transition to free weights much easier and safer; and (3) it will provide you with confidence before using free weights, as all of these exercises will be rather easy for you to perform. Another benefit of performing these exercises is that they all can be done at home with virtually no (or little) equipment.

You will notice that the order of the exercises suggested in this chapter works your larger muscles first, then proceeds to the smaller muscles, working your abdominals last. This philosophy follows the principles outlined in the summary section of chapter 2. Be sure to read these guidelines regularly, as you should be following all of these principles when you train, whether using free weights or your body weight for resistance.

Use the following training schedule to start your strength-training program. It will take you eight weeks to complete, and you should notice positive strength and performance changes at its conclusion. Each exercise is described in detail later in this chapter.

Strength-Training Routines

TRADITIONAL SINGLE SETS

During weeks 1 and 2, perform 3 sets of each exercise for 8–12 repetitions before moving on to the next exercise. For example, perform a set of wall slides, rest for about one minute and then perform your second set. Exercise three times per week.

Week 1

Day 1	**Day 2**	**Day 3**
Wall Slide	Squat Jumps	Wall Slide
Vertical Jump	Heel Raises	Vertical Jump
Pull-ups	Pull-ups	Pull-ups
Push-ups—Regular	Push-ups—Incline	Push-ups—Decline
Chin-ups	Chin-ups	Chin-ups
Dips— Feet on Floor	Dips— Feet Elevated	Dips— Feet on Floor
Abdominals	Abdominals	Abdominals

Week 2

Day 1	**Day 2**	**Day 3**
Squat Jumps	Wall Slide	Squat Jumps
Heel Raises	Vertical Jump	Heel Raises
Pull-ups	Pull-ups	Pull-ups
Push-ups—Regular	Push-ups—Incline	Push-ups—Decline
Chin-ups	Chin-ups	Chin-ups
Dips— Feet Elevated	Dips— Feet on Floor	Dips— Feet Elevated
Abdominals	Abdominals	Abdominals

SUPER SETS

During weeks 3 and 4 group your exercises together, performing super sets. Your goal still should be to train 8–12 repetitions for each set while performing 3 sets of each exercise. Perform your super sets as shown by the exercise grouping. For example, perform a set of wall slides followed immediately by vertical jumps; then rest until you are recovered (about 1 minute) and repeat for your second set. Exercise three days per week.

Week 3

Day 1	**Day 2**	**Day 3**
Wall Slide Vertical Jump	Squat Jumps Heel Raises	Wall Slide Vertical Jump
Pull-ups Chin-ups	Pull-ups Chin-ups	Pull-ups Chin-ups

Push-ups—Regular
Dips—
   Feet on Floor
	Push-ups—Incline
	Dips—
	   Feet Elevated
		Push-ups—Decline
		Dips—
		   Feet on Floor

Abdominals	Abdominals	Abdominals

Week 4

Day 1	**Day 2**	**Day 3**
Squat Jumps Heel Raises	Wall Slides Vertical Jump	Squat Jumps Heel Raises
Pull-ups Chin-ups	Pull-ups Chin-ups	Pull-ups Chin-ups

Push-ups—Regular
Dips—
   Feet Elevated
	Push-ups—Incline
	Dips—
	   Feet on Floor
		Push-ups—Decline
		Dips—
		   Feet Elevated

Abdominals	Abdominals	Abdominals

CIRCUIT TRAINING

During the next month (weeks 5–8) you can increase your muscular endurance and strength by performing your exercises in a circuit format. With 8–12 repetitions for each exercise, you should work your way through all six exercises, performing one set of each and resting for 30 seconds between them. Perform three circuits in this manner, finishing your exercise session with abdominal exercises.

Week 5

Day 1	Day 2	Day 3
Wall Slide	Squat Jumps	Wall Slide
Vertical Jump	Heel raises	Vertical Jump
Pull-ups	Pull-ups	Pull-ups
Push-ups—Regular	Push-ups—Incline	Push-ups—Decline
Chin-ups	Chin-ups	Chin-ups
Dips— Feet on Floor	Dips— Feet Elevated	Dips— Feet on Floor
Abdominals	Abdominals	Abdominals

Week 6

Day 1	Day 2	Day 3
Squat Jumps	Wall Slide	Squat Jumps
Heel Raises	Vertical Jump	Heel Raises
Pull-ups	Pull-ups	Pull-ups
Push-ups—Regular	Push-ups—Incline	Push-ups—Decline
Chin-ups	Chin-ups	Chin-ups
Dips— Feet Elevated	Dips— Feet on Floor	Dips— Feet Elevated
Abdominals	Abdominals	Abdominals

Week 7 (Same as Week 5)

Week 8 (Same as Week 6)

Record your daily repetitions on Form 5-1. This will enable you to monitor your daily and weekly progress. A copy of this form has been included in "Appendix A" so that you can remove it from the book to make copies as you need them.

Each of the aforementioned exercises is described in detail in the next section of this chapter. Be sure to use proper training techniques for each exercise in combination with the guidelines presented in the summary for chapter 2.

At the end of your two-month program turn back to chapter 4 and measure your physical performance levels again. I am sure you will be pleased with the results.

Form 5-1. Daily Workout Recorder

NAME _____

DATE												
EXERCISES	REPS	REPS	REPS	REPS	REPS	REPS	REPS	REPS	REPS	REPS	REPS	REPS

Strength-Training Exercises

EXERCISES FOR THE LOWER BODY

WALL SLIDE

This exercise strengthens the muscles in your thighs and hips. It is a favorite exercise among skiers and strengthens muscles which are used in a variety of sports.

Start the exercise by assuming the position shown in illustration 5-1. Your feet should be spread slightly wider than shoulder width and placed 12–18 inches away from the wall. Your back, neck and head should rest against the wall to prevent any stress to these areas. Your hands can be placed against the wall for balance.

To perform a repetition slowly lower your body toward the floor by bending your knees. Move slowly and under control, breathing in as you do so. Your upper body should stay pressed against the wall for support and proper body alignment. When your thighs are parallel to the floor (illustration 5-2) pause and then press your body back into the starting position by pushing with your legs. Exhale as you exert force, pushing your body upward.

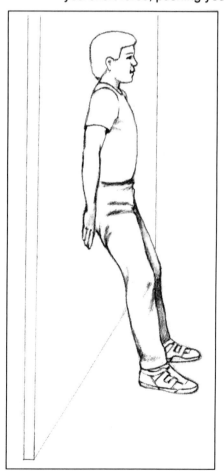

Illustration 5-1

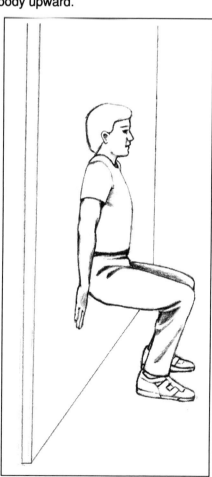

Illustration 5-2

VERTICAL JUMP

The vertical jump also will build strength in the thighs and hips but will do so in a more explosive manner than the wall slide. This exercise has direct application to a number of sport skills.

Start the vertical jump by assuming the position in illustration 5-3; knees slightly bent, hands down at your side, ready to explode into an upward jump. When you are ready, jump as high into the air as you can, reaching up with one hand. Quickly recover and jump again, reaching up with the other hand.

You might try reaching for an object or mark on the wall when you jump as a means for monitoring your progress from one exercise session to the next.

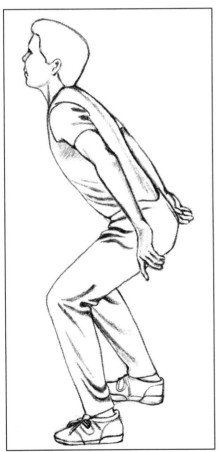

Illustration 5-3

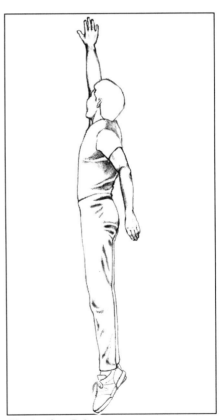

Illustration 5-4

SQUAT JUMP

The squat jump is another explosive exercise for the thigh and hip regions which will directly apply to a number of sport activities. Start the squat jump by assuming the position in illustration 5-5. Notice that the thighs are parallel to the floor. The back, neck and head are in straight alignment, and the hands are held behind the head; elbows high. Start with the left foot held forward as shown and jump as high as you can (illustration 5-6). When you land, switch the forward foot and do not let the thighs drop below your knees.

Illustration 5-5

Illustration 5-6

HEEL RAISES

Heel raises strengthen the muscles of the lower leg. Start this exercise by balancing your body as shown in illustration 5-7 or supporting yourself against the wall. Tuck your right foot in behind your left leg, supporting all of your weight on your left leg. Pressing the toes of your left foot to the floor, elevate your body upward, raising your left heel in the process. When you get to the top, pause and then lower your heel back to the floor. Perform your desired number of repetitions and then switch feet.

Illustration 5-7

Illustration 5-8

EXERCISES FOR THE UPPER BODY

PULL-UPS

Pull-ups will strengthen the muscles in your upper back and arms. To start this exercise hang from a bar with your palms facing away from you as in illustration 5-9. Using only your arms, pull your chin up until it passes just over the bar. Pause and then lower yourself to the starting position again.

Illustration 5-9

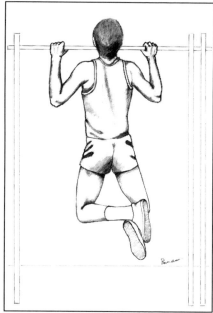

Illustration 5-10

PUSH-UPS

Push-ups are a fantastic exercise for strengthening the muscles of the chest and the backs of the upper arms. This exercise can be slightly modified using a variety of positions so that the chest muscles are thoroughly stimulated.

Perform the *regular push-up* by assuming the position in illustration 5-11. Notice that the back, neck and head are in perfect alignment. Keep this position throughout the entire movement to protect your low back. Lower yourself to the floor as in illustration 5-12 and then press your body back up into the starting position, completing the movement.

The *incline push-up* is performed in a similar fashion to the regular push-up with the exception that your body is positioned at an incline with your upper body held higher than your lower. This can easily be accomplished using chairs as shown in illustration 5-13 and 5-14. Positioning your body in such a manner will stimulate the upper portion of your chest muscles more than regular push-ups.

Decline push-ups do just the opposite, stimulating the lower portion of your chest. To perform this exercise elevate your feet approximately 12–18 inches off the floor and perform a push-up as you normally would. Illustrations 5-15 and 5-16 show this position.

Illustration 5-11

Illustration 5-12

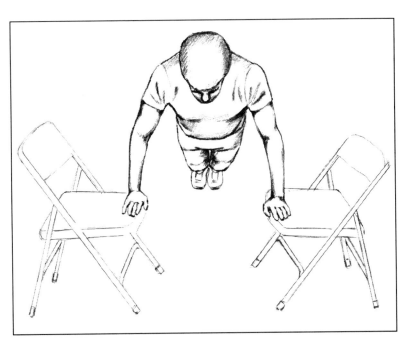

Illustration 5-13

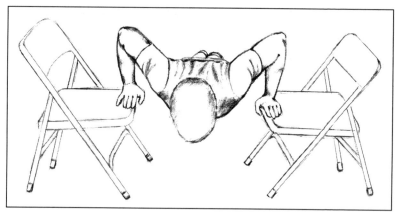

Illustration 5-14

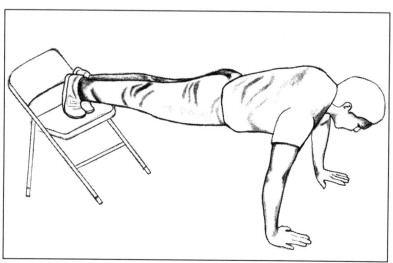

Illustration 5-15

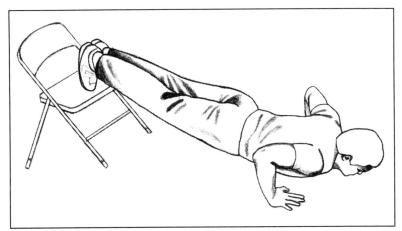

Illustration 5-16

CHIN-UPS

Chin-ups are similar to pull-ups with the exception that the hands are turned so that your palms face you, instead of away from you. Also, you probably will find it more comfortable to keep your hands closer together than you did when performing pull-ups. Like pull-ups, chin-ups work the muscles of your back but they also concentrate on strengthening your biceps or the muscles on the front of your upper arms.

Use illustrations 5-9 and 5-10 as a guide, making the suggested hand changes.

DIPS

Dips will strengthen the muscles of your chest and the muscles on the back of your upper arm. Dips can be performed using two chairs for support, or three chairs to create variety. Illustration 5-17 depicts the starting position for dips with your feet on the ground. illustration 5-18 shows the "dip" phase of this exercise. By lowering your body between the chairs you get a good stretch of your chest and arm muscles. Pause, and then press your body back up into the starting position.

A variation of this exercise can be performed by having your feet elevated as shown in illustration 5-19.

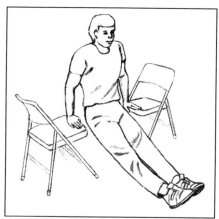

Illustration 5-17

Illustration 5-18

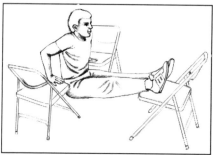

Illustration 5-19

EXERCISES FOR THE ABDOMINALS

The muscles of the abdominal wall and the low back work together to create stability in the midtorso region. These muscles provide support in keeping the upper body properly aligned over the lower body, thus reducing the pressure on your low spine. They also offer protection for vital organs housed within your abdominal cavity. These two muscle groups work together in rotation type movements and sport skills such as hitting, throwing and other twisting and turning type activities.

To maximally train these muscles, you should choose a variety of abdominal exercises, as well as exercises for your low back (chapter 6). Do not be concerned with the number of repetitions you perform, but rather perform your movements with strict form and the highest possible intensity. Concentrate on each repetition and contract your muscles with the greatest force possible. You will perform fewer reps but get more out of your training.

Be sure to keep your low back flat at all times by performing a pelvic tilt prior to each repetition. A pelvic tilt is described below.

CRUNCH EXERCISES (FLEXION)

The rectus abdominus muscles can be exercised using a variety of calisthenic exercises such as the ones which follow.

Pelvic Tilts

Position yourself as in illustration 5-20. Your knees should be bent and your back and neck muscles completely relaxed. Tighten your abdominal and buttock muscles so that your hips rotate forward and up, flattening your low back in the process. Hold this position for 6 seconds and then relax. The movement is very small and the low back should only flatten, not actually come off the floor.

Set the tilt position prior to performing any of the other abdominal crunch activities.

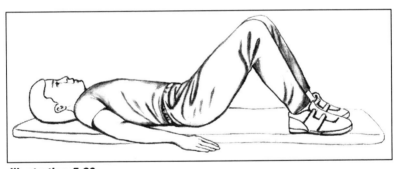

Illustration 5-20

Classic Crunch

Start this exercise by performing a pelvic tilt with your hands placed on your abdomen. Keep your feet and back pressed to the floor. Curl up, crunching your abdominal muscles as you raise your shoulder blades off the floor. You may wish to use a variety of hand and/or arm positions when you perform this movement. But avoid placing your hands behind your head and pulling on your neck as you curl up. Either use your hands to support your neck or keep them in front of your body.

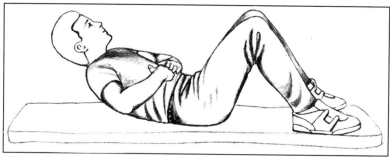

Illustration 5-21

Advanced Crunch

Position yourself as in illustration 5-21. Hands should be behind your neck for support, knees bent and ankles crossed. Curl up, bringing your upper torso toward your knees without pulling on your neck (illustration 5-23). You can maximize the effect of this exercise if you pull your knees in toward your upper body as you curl up, and then let them drift away from you as you lower your upper torso back to the floor. Do not let them drift farther than your hips, however (keep knees over hips), as this will place a strain on your low back.

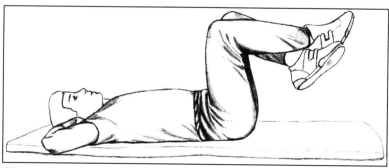

Illustration 5-22

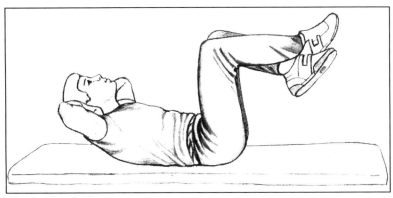

Illustration 5-23

Knee To Chest

Support your low back by placing your hands under your buttocks. Your legs should be bent as much as possible, with your knees and ankles together. Using your lower abdominal muscles, pull your knees up toward your chest until your buttocks actually lift off the ground (illustration 5-24). Avoid using momentum to accomplish this action, but rather make your movements slow and deliberate. Be sure to resist gravity as the feet return to the floor, touching your feet lightly before starting the next repetition.

Illustration 5-24

ROTARY EXERCISES (ROTATION)

The internal and external oblique muscles are responsible for rotation of the upper torso over the lower. As with the flexion exercises, the obliques can be trained either with the use of machines or with calisthenic exercises like those illustrated below.

Single-Side Rotation (knee bent)

Assume the position in illustration 5-25. The left foot should be placed flat on the ground with the knee bent at approximately a 90° angle. Your right ankle should be placed on your left knee. Place your left hand behind your neck and either rest your right hand on your abdomen or on the floor next to your right hip.

Curl up and rotate so that you touch your right knee with your left elbow. Pause and contract the abdominal muscles before returning to the floor.

When you have completed your desired number of repetitions, be sure to switch legs and work the other side.

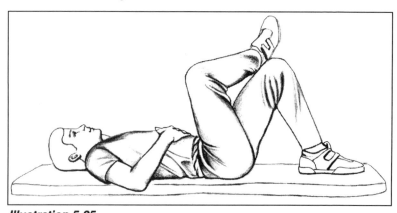

Illustration 5-25

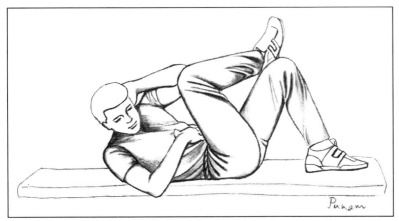

Illustration 5-26

Advanced Rotational Crunch

This exercise is identical to the advanced crunch with the exception that you should rotate as you curl up, reaching for the left knee with the right elbow on odd numbered repetitions, and reaching for the right knee with the left elbow on even numbered repetitions.

Advanced Single-Side Rotation (knee straight)

Assume the position in illustration 5-27. Your left knee should be bent at a 90° angle with your foot flat on the ground. Your right leg is held out straight and your left arm is held straight back on the floor. Initiate the curl-up and rotation by bringing the right leg and left arm up together until they meet.

Move slowly and under control to avoid pulling your hamstring muscles. The left shoulder blade should rise up off the floor as you reach out over your right foot. Pause, then return to the floor.

When you have completed your desired number of repetitions, switch legs and repeat.

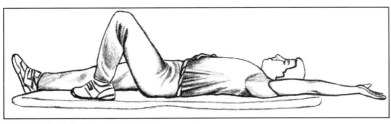

Illustration 5-27

Illustration 5-28

VI. Weight Training Exercises and Routines

This chapter contains weight training exercises and progressive routines for the beginner.

Look at the photographs for each exercise and read the accompanying directions. It is important to lift properly if you want to get the most results for your efforts. Perform each movement under control. Stretch your muscles at both the start and the finish of each repetition. Perform each movement fully. Do not bounce, swing or cheat. Always move slowly and control the weight. You are in charge!

Beginning, intermediate and advanced level exercises are presented. By following the suggested routines at the end of the chapter you will be able to progress naturally and safely. Change routines every six weeks until you have performed them all. At that time, you can create your own routines but remember to train all your major muscle groups. Don't just use your favorite exercises.

Although exercises are presented by muscle groups, you may actually use several muscle groups when performing a given exercise. Exercises are therefore grouped by the major muscle group which is stimulated.

Breathe freely when you perform these exercises. You should breathe in during the relaxation phase of each repetition, and breathe out during the work phase. For example, when you perform a bench press you should breathe in as you lower the bar to your chest and breathe out as you press. Avoid holding your breath as this could cause you to pass out.

Remember, quality training techniques will lead to quality results!

Exercises

LEGS

Squats. (Thighs and buttocks). Place the bar across the back of your shoulders at the base of your neck. Space your hands evenly on the bar for balance. Your feet should be slightly wider than shoulder width apart. Lower yourself until your thighs are parallel to the floor, then return to a standing position. Do not bounce but move slowly and under control. Keep your back straight and your head up throughout the movement.

Photo 6-2

Photo 6-1

Leg Press. (Thighs and buttocks). Adjust the chair so that your legs are at a right angle (90°) as shown in photo 6-3. Place your feet firmly against the pedals. Keep your buttocks and back pressed firmly down into the chair. Hold on to the handles at the side of the chair for extra balance and support. Straighten your legs until they are fully extended but not locked. Lower the weights and repeat. Do not let the weights slam down, but rather control them and let them touch lightly.

Photo 6-3

Photo 6-4

Leg Extension. (Thighs). In a sitting position, place your feet behind the roller pads, point your toes back toward you and drape your lower legs so your knees are snug against the table. Keeping your back straight, straighten your legs. Pause. Lower the resistance and repeat. If you are using weight boots (photo 6-7) you can perform this exercise one leg at a time.

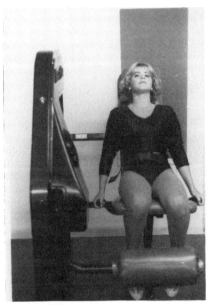

Photo 6-5

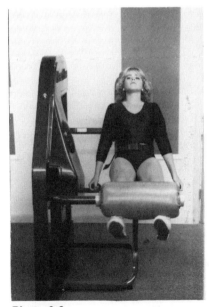

Photo 6-6

Photo 6-7

Leg Curl. (Thighs). Lie face down on the table and place your heels under the roller pads with your toes pointed downward. Your knees should be positioned so they are just off the table. Contract the muscles in your buttocks and press your hips downward into the table. Keep them there throughout the exercise. Curl your legs until the roller pads touch your buttocks. Pause. Lower the resistance until the weights lightly touch, and then repeat. If you are wearing weight boots (photo 6-10) you can perform this exercise one leg at a time.

Photo 6-8

Photo 6-9

Photo 6-10

Heel Raise. (Lower Legs). Place a barbell across the back of your shoulders (photo 6-11) or across your thighs (photo 6-12). Elevate your toes by placing them on a 2" by 4" wood strip or two barbell plates. Rise up onto your toes and pause. Then lower your heels to the ground and repeat.

Photo 6-11

Photo 6-12

Photo 6-13

CHEST

Bench Press. (Chest, shoulders, upper arms). Lie on your bench (photo 6-14). Your knees should be bent at right angles (90°) and your feet should be placed firmly on the ground. Your lower back and buttocks should be pressed down onto the bench throughout the entire exercise movement. Grasp the bar where your hands feel most comfortable. This probably will be slightly wider than shoulder width apart. Lower the bar to your chest, pause, and then press it up until your arms straighten. Repeat. Be careful to move slowly and under control. Do not bounce the bar off your chest but merely touch it lightly to your chest. **You always should use a spotter for this exercise!**

Photo 6-14   **Photo 6-15**

Incline Press. (Chest, shoulders and upper arm). This exercise is similar to the bench press. The major difference is the angle of the bench. By angling the bench at about 45° you permit the upper chest to be stimulated more than during the regular bench press. You can either use dumbbells or a barbell for this exercise. Grasp the barbell or dumbbells so your hands are spaced slightly wider than shoulder width apart.

Photo 6-16

Photo 6-17

Pull-overs. (Chest, shoulders, back). Lie flat on your bench (photo 6-18). Bend your knees at right angles (90°) and place your feet firmly on the ground. Your buttocks and lower back should be pressed down against the bench. Bend your arms slightly and reach back, grasping the bar with your hands just slightly wider than shoulder width apart. Pull the bar up over your chest, pause, and then return it to the floor. Move slowly so that you give the muscles in your chest a good stretch. Use a weight light enough so that you do not need to cheat by bending your elbows.

Photo 6-18   *Photo 6-19*

Dumbbell Flies. (Chest and shoulders). Lie flat on your bench with a dumbbell in each hand. Bend your elbows slightly. Lower the dumbbells down to your side, just lower than the bench, until you get a good stretch in your chest muscles. Bring the dumbbells up toward each other, stopping when they line up over your shoulders. This position will maintain tension in your chest muscles. Lower the dumbbells and repeat the movement. (If this exercise is performed on the incline bench it will stimulate your upper chest muscles.)

Photo 6-20   *Photo 6-21*

Parallel Bar Dips. (Chest, shoulders, upper arms). This is a fantastic upper body exercise, especially for the lower chest muscles. Using two parallel bars which are slightly wider than your shoulders, support yourself with your arms straight. Lean slightly forward throughout the exercise. Lower your body until your shoulders almost touch the bars. Pause. Press yourself back up into a straight arm support and then repeat the exercise again.

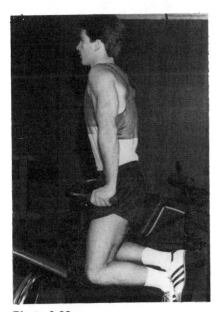
Photo 6-22

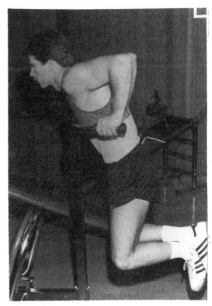
Photo 6-23

As you get stronger you may need to add resistance to your body when you perform this movement. Simply hang an extra barbell plate from your waist as you do your dips.

BACK

Bent-over Rowing. (Back and upper arms). Stand with your feet slightly wider than shoulder width apart. Bend your knees slightly. Your upper torso should be parallel to the ground. Grasp the bar slightly wider than shoulder width and pull it up toward you until it touches your chest. Pause. Then lower the bar and repeat. Do not jerk the weight up by using your body; only use the muscles of your back and arms. Move the weight slowly and under control. This exercise can also be performed with a dumbbell, exercising one arm at a time.

Photo 6-24   **Photo 6-25**

Seated Row. (Back and upper arms). Sit with your legs extended, back straight. You should sit far enough away from the weight machine so that there is constant tension on the cable. Hold the cable handles or bar about shoulder width apart. Pull the cable into your stomach without letting your upper body lean either forward or backward. Only use the muscles in your back and upper arms. Pause when your stomach is touched by the cable handles or bar. Let your arms stretch out again and repeat the movement.

Photo 6-26   **Photo 6-27**

Lat Pulldown. (Back and shoulders). To start this exercise, grasp the bar with your hands as wide apart as possible. Kneel or sit down so that you keep tension on the cable when your arms are fully extended. Pull the bar down behind your neck until it touches the top of your shoulders. Pause. Let your arms stretch up again until they are fully extended and repeat. You may need to have a partner hold you down when you perform this exercise so the weights do not pull you off the floor.

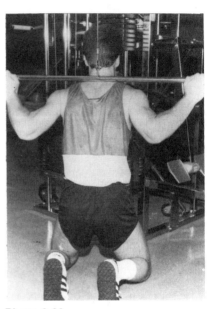

Photo 6-28   **Photo 6-29**

Photo 6-30

Pull-ups. (Back and shoulders). Grasp the pull-up bar with your palms facing away from you. Hang in a fully extended position (photo 6-30). Pull your body upward until either your chin clears the bar (photo 6-31) or until the back of your neck touches the bar (photo 6-32). Pause. Lower yourself to full extension again and repeat. By alternating your touch positions, either chin or neck, and changing the width of your grip, you can develop your back muscles from a wide variety of angles. As you get stronger, you may also want to hang weights from your body for added resistance as you did with your parallel bar dips.

Photo 6-31

Photo 6-32

Shoulder Shrugs. (Back). Grasp two dumbbells with your palms facing in. Let them hang at your side (photo 6-33). Using only the muscles in your upper back, pull your shoulders up toward your ears. Pause. Lower your shoulders and repeat.

Photo 6-33

Photo 6-34

Upright Rowing. (Back and upper arms). Hold the barbell using a grip which is slightly less than shoulder width. Pull the bar up toward your chin until your thumbs touch your armpits. Do not use your body to jerk up the weight; use only the muscles of your back and upper arms. When the bar has been fully raised, pause. Lower the bar and repeat.

Photo 6-35

Photo 6-36

Back Hyperextension. (Back). This is a two-part exercise and will require the help of a training partner if you are to perform it correctly. Lie on the floor face down with your hands clasped behind your head. Have your partner hold down your lower legs. Slowly raise your chest and chin off the floor while keeping your hips pressed firmly to the ground. Pause in this raised position, then lower your body and repeat. Be sure to keep your head and neck straight as you should not extend both your neck and back at the same time.

The second part of this exercise requires that your partner hold your shoulders down (photo 6-38). Perform this portion of the exercise with one leg at a time. Tighten the buttock of your right leg, and with the leg fully extended and straightened, lift it off the floor as high as possible. Your hips should again be pressed against the floor. Pause when you have it fully lifted, then lower and repeat this movement 8–12 times with the same leg. After you have finished with your right leg, switch and exercise your left side.

Photo 6-37

Photo 6-38

SHOULDERS

Standing Military Press. (Shoulders and upper arms). Bring the barbell to a position where it rests on the upper portion of your chest (photo 6-39). Grasp the bar with your hands slightly wider than shoulder width apart. Press the bar upward over your head until your arms are fully extended. Lower the bar to the level of the top of your shoulders and press again. Be sure you let the muscles

Photo 6-39

Photo 6-40

of your shoulders and upper arms do the work. Do not use the muscles of your legs to help you get the weight up. Keep your back straight throughout the entire movement.

This exercise also may be performed in a sitting position using either dumbbells or a barbell (photos 6-41–6-44). You also may desire to exercise your muscles from a slightly different angle by bringing the bar down behind your neck (photo 6-44). This is referred to as a posterior press.

Photo 6-41

Photo 6-42

Photo 6-43

Photo 6-44

Photo 6-45

Photo 6-46

Photo 6-47

Lateral Dumbbell Raise. (Shoulders). Stand or sit with a dumbbell in each hand, arms hanging down, palms turned in. Slightly bend your elbow. Using your shoulder muscles, raise your arms to the sides, bringing the dumbbells up over your head until they are straight above your shoulders. Pause. Then lower the dumbbells and repeat.

Forward Dumbbell Raise. (Shoulders). This exercise is similar to the lateral dumbbell raise, except that the dumbbells are raised to the overhead position by bringing them up in front of the body (photo 6-47).

Bent-over Lateral Raise. (Shoulders). Bend over at your waist so that your upper torso is parallel to the floor. Spread your feet apart slightly wider than shoulder width to provide balance, and keep a slight bend in your knees to protect your back. Raise the dumbbells to either side until they reach shoulder height with your palms facing down. Pause in this position and then lower the weights so that your arms are fully extended and hanging below your body. Be sure to keep a slight bend in your elbows but let your shoulders do all the work, not your arms.

Photo 6-48   *Photo 6-49*

ARMS

Tricep Extension. (Upper arm—back portion). This exercise may be performed either standing or sitting. Grasp a dumbbell with both hands and hold it above your head with your arms fully extended. Keep your elbows pointed upward and inward while lowering the dumbbell as far as you can. Pause in the downward position and then slowly press the dumbbell back to the overhead position.

Photo 6-50

Photo 6-51

French Dumbbell Curl. (Upper arm—back portion). Hold a dumbbell in one hand and your arm fully extended overhead. Keep your elbow pointed upward. Bend your elbow, lowering the dumbbell to the middle of your back. Pause in this position and then return the dumbbell to the starting position. Be sure to exercise both arms.

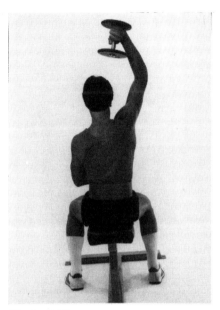

Photo 6-52   *Photo 6-53*

Close Grip Bench Press. (Upper arm, chest, shoulders). This exercise is identical to the regular bench press, except that your hands should be much closer together. With this close grip you stimulate the backs of your upper arms and your inner chest muscles. Be sure to keep your back pressed flat against the bench throughout the movement and also keep your feet planted firmly on the ground.

Photo 6-54

Photo 6-55

Barbell Curl. (Upper arm—front portion). Stand with your feet slightly more than shoulder width apart. Grasp the bar from underneath and lift it to your thighs (photo 6-56). Space your hands so they are slightly closer than shoulder width. By bending your elbows, curl the bar until it touches your shoulders. Do not swing your upper body to help lift the barbell; only use your arms. Lower the weight slowly to the starting position and make sure you fully extend your arms in this downward position. Repeat this movement slowly and under control until you have performed your desired number of repetitions.

Photo 6-56

Photo 6-57

Preacher Curl. (Upper arm—front portion). Rest the upper portion of your arms on the preacher bench (photo 6-58). Fully extend your arms and grasp the bar with your palms facing up. Curl the bar up to your shoulders while keeping your arms pressed against the preacher bench. Remain seated throughout the entire movement. Pause in the upward position (photo 6-59) and then slowly

Photo 6-58

lower the bar to the starting position. Make sure you fully extend your arms at the completion of the movement. Repeat.

Photo 6-59

Incline Dumbbell Curl. (Upper arm—front portion). Use your incline bench for this exercise. Hold the dumbbells with your palms facing away and let them hang down at your sides. By bending at the elbows curl the dumbbells up to your shoulder. You can either curl both dumbbells at once or curl them alternately. Return the dumbbell to the hanging position and make sure your arm is fully extended, giving your upper arm muscles a good stretch. Be sure to keep your back flat against the bench throughout the entire exercise.

Photo 6-60

Photo 6-61

Concentration Curl. (Upper arm—front portion). Sit on a bench with your legs spread comfortably apart. Rest your right elbow on the inner portion of your right thigh and hold a dumbbell in your right hand with your arm fully extended. Curl the dumbbell to your right shoulder while keeping your elbow pressed firmly against your thigh. Return the dumbbell to a hanging position with your arm fully extended and repeat the movement. Be sure to exercise your left arm too.

Photo 6-62

Photo 6-63

Reverse Barbell Curl. (Upper arm—front portion and lower arm). This exercise is identical to the regular barbell curl except the grip is reversed. When the bar is held against your thighs, your palms should be facing your body.

Photo 6-64

Wrist Curl. (Lower arm). Sit on a bench with your legs spread about shoulder width apart. Drape your wrists and hands just off your knees (photo 6-65). While holding the bar relax your wrists and let the bar pull your hands down as far as possible. From this position curl your wrists, raising the bar up above your knees. This exercise can be performed with your palms facing either toward or away from you.

Photo 6-65

Photo 6-66

Exercise Routines

The following exercise routines will help you progress from simple exercises to more advanced exercise routines in a progressive and systematic manner. If your training site does not have the necessary equipment to perform a particular exercise, merely substitute another exercise which works the same body part.

These nine routines will carry you through a year of training as you rotate routines every six weeks.

The column headed "Chapter-Photo" locates the photos pertaining to each exercise. For each photo, the first number is the chapter number and the second number is the photo or illustration number.

Example: **"Leg Press 6-3, 6-4"** indicates that the photos for the leg press are photos 3 and 4 in chapter 6.

ROUTINE # 1

Exercise	Chapter-Photo
Squats	6-1, 6-2
Leg Curl	6-8, 6-9, 6-10
Heel Raises	6-11, 6-12, 6-13
Bench Press	6-14, 6-15
Bent-over Rowing	6-24, 6-25
Standing Military Press	6-39, 6-40
Upright Rowing	6-35, 6-36
Tricep Extension	6-50, 6-51
Barbell curl	6-56, 6-57
Wrist Curl (palms up)	6-65, 6-66
Pelvic Tilt	5-20

ROUTINE # 2

Exercise	Chapter-Photo
Leg Press	6-3, 6-4
Leg Curl	6-8, 6-9, 6-10
Heel Raises	6-11, 6-12, 6-13
Incline Press	6-16, 6-17
Seated Row	6-26, 6-27
Seated Posterior Press	6-43, 6-44
Shoulder Shrugs	6-33, 6-34
French Dumbbell Curl	6-52, 6-53
Concentration Curl	6-62, 6-63
Wrist Curl (palms down)	6-65, 6-66
Classic Crunch	5-22, 5-23

ROUTINE # 3

Exercise	Chapter-Photo
Squats	6-1, 6-2
Leg Curl	6-8, 6-9, 6-10
Leg Extension	6-5, 6-6, 6-7
Heel Raises	6-11, 6-12, 6-13
Bench Press	6-14, 6-15
Lat Pulldown	6-28, 6-29
Seated Dumbbell Press	6-41, 6-42
Close Grip Bench Press	6-54, 6-55
Preacher Curl	6-58, 6-59
Reverse Barbell Curl	6-64
Knee to Chest	5-24
Single-side Rotation (knee bent)	5-25, 5-26

ROUTINE # 4

Exercise	Chapter-Photo
Leg Press	6-3, 6-4
Leg Curl	6-8, 6-9, 6-10
Leg Extension	6-5, 6-6, 6-7
Heel Raises	6-11, 6-12, 6-13
Incline Press	6-16, 6-17
Bent-over Rowing (with Barbell)	6-24, 6-25
Dumbell Flies	6-20, 6-21
Shoulder Shrugs	6-33, 6-34
Standing Military Press	6-39, 6-40
Back Hyperextension	6-37, 6-38
Incline Dumbbell Curl	6-60, 6-61
Wrist Curl (palms up)	6-65, 6-66
Advanced Crunch	5-23, 5-25
Advanced Single-side Rotation (knee straight)	5-27

ROUTINE # 5

Exercise	Chapter-Photo
Squats	6-1, 6-2
Leg Curl	6-8, 6-9, 6-10
Leg Extension	6-5, 6-6, 6-7
Heel Raises	6-11, 6-12, 6-13
Bench Press	6-14, 6-15
Seated Row	6-26, 6-27
Parallel Bar Dips	6-22, 6-23
Lat Pulldown	6-28, 6-29
Seated Posterior Press	6-43, 6-44
Barbell Curl	6-56, 6-57
Tricep Extension	6-50, 6-51
Reverse Barbell Curl	6-64
Pelvic Tilt	5-20
Knee to Chest	5-24

ROUTINE # 6

Exercise	Chapter-Photo
Leg Press	6-3, 6-4
Leg Curl	6-8, 6-9, 6-10
Leg Extension	6-5, 6-6, 6-7
Heel Raises	6-11, 6-12, 6-13
Incline Press	6-16, 6-17
Bent-over Rowing	6-24, 6-25
Pull-over	6-18, 6-19
Seated Dumbbell Press	6-41, 6-42
Upright Rowing	6-35, 6-36
French Dumbbell Curl	6-52, 6-53
Concentration Curls	6-62, 6-63
Wrist Curl (palms down)	6-65, 6-66
Classic Crunch	5-21
Single-side Rotation (knee bent)	5-25, 5-26

ROUTINE # 7

Exercises	**Chapter-Photo**
Squats	6-1, 6-2
Leg Curl	6-8, 6-9, 6-10
Leg Extension	6-5, 6-6, 6-7
Heel Raises	6-11, 6-12, 6-13
Bench Press	6-14, 6-15
Lat Pulldown	6-28, 6-29
Parallel Bar Dips	6-22, 6-23
Seated Row	6-26, 6-27
Standing Military Press	6-39, 6-40
Shoulder Shrugs	6-33, 6-34
Close Grip Bench Press	6-54, 6-55
Preacher Curl	6-58, 6-59
Reverse Barbell Curl	6-64
Advanced Crunch	5-22, 5-23
Advanced Single-side Rotation (knee bent)	5-27

ROUTINE # 8

Exercise	**Chapter-Photo**

(These exercises should be performed in super sets by group)

Squats	6-1, 6-2
Pull-overs	6-18, 6-19
Leg Curl	6-8, 6-9, 6-10
Heel Raises	6-11, 6-12, 6-13
Back Hyperextension	6-37, 6-38
Bench Press	6-14, 6-15
Parallel Bar Dips	6-22, 6-23
Dumbbell Flies	6-20, 6-21

Seated Row	6-26, 6-27
Pull-ups	6-30, 6-31, 6-32
Upright Rowing	6-35, 6-36
Lateral Dumbbell Raises	6-45, 6-46
Forward Dumbbell Raises	6-47
Bent-over Lateral Raise	6-48, 6-49
Barbell Curl	6-56, 6-57
Concentration Curl	6-62, 6-63
Pelvic Tilt	5-20
Knee to Chest	5-24

ROUTINE # 9

Exercise   **Chapter-Photo**

(These exercises should be performed in super sets by group)

Leg Press	6-3, 6-4
Leg Extension	6-5, 6-6, 6-7
Dumbbell Flies	6-20, 6-21
Leg Curl	6-8, 6-9, 6-10
Heel Raises	6-11, 6-12, 6-13
Back Hyperextension	6-37, 6-38
Pull-overs	6-18, 6-19
Incline Press	6-16, 6-17
Close Grip Bench Press	6-54, 6-55
Bent-over Rowing	6-24, 6-25
Lat Pulldown	6-28, 6-29
Shoulder Shrugs	6-33, 6-34

Standing Military Press	6-39, 6-40
Seated Dumbbell Press	6-41, 6-42
Bent-over Lateral Raise	6-48, 6-49
Preacher Curl	6-58, 6-59
Incline Dumbbell Curl	6-60, 6-61
Classic Crunch	5-21
Single-side Rotation (knee bent)	5-25, 5-26

Summary

Follow the routines outlined in this chapter and you will experience positive changes in flexibility, muscular strength and muscular endurance. Change training routines every six weeks to avoid boredom and to thoroughly develop your musculature. Remember to reassess the fitness components outlined in chapter 4 every twelve weeks, because the improvements you notice will help motivate you to continue with your strength training.

You also can get motivation on a daily basis by recording your repetitions and weights during each workout. Not only will you feel encouraged when you notice increases in repetitions and weight, but you also will be able to quickly see how many repetitions you need in a particular exercise to increase for that day or set. Table 6-1 was designed for this purpose. This chart will allow you to record your exercises, as well as your repetitions and weight for each of your three sets, on any given day. This table is also located in the appendix so that you can remove it to make copies for future use.

Table 6-1. Daily Workout Recorder.

NAME _____

DATE												
EXERCISES	WT / REPS	WT / REPS	WT / REPS	WT / REPS	WT / REPS	WT / REPS	WT / REPS	WT / REPS	WT / REPS	WT / REPS	WT / REPS	WT / REPS

VII. Competitive Weight-Lifting Opportunities

The world of weight lifting goes beyond providing a means by which to train for strength. Weight-lifting is a sport in itself. Competitions are held in three areas: body building, power lifting and Olympic lifting.

These competitions are arranged by age group. The power lifting and Olympic lifting competitions are structured further by weight classes. This provides everyone with an equal opportunity to succeed.

Body Building

The sport of body building is designed for those individuals interested in sculpturing their muscles, much the way an artist might sculpture a figure out of rock. The body builder must work to increase muscular size while retaining as much definition as possible in every muscle. Symmetry or balance also is very important. The body builder must develop each muscle group to its fullest capability rather than just developing certain favorite muscle groups.

Competitions are held for teenagers in this sport. You can write to AAU House, 3400 West 86th Street, Indianapolis, IN 46268, if you would like more information concerning contests or opportunities in your area. This organization oversees the Mr. America contest, as well as the Junior Mr. America contest in the United States. The International Federation of Body Builders is also involved in the organization of body-building contests. They may be contacted at International Federation of Body Builders, 2875 Bates Road, Montreal, Quebec H3F 1B7, for further information.

Power Lifting

The sport of power lifting in this country is governed by the United States Power Federation (USPF), although there is an international federation as well. Power-lifting contests require the competitor to participate in three lifts: the squat, the bench press and the dead lift. Each lifter is given three opportunities for each of these lifts, and the heaviest lift for each exercise is counted toward the total score.

The USPF has developed programs for individuals 14 and older. Competitions also are held for teenagers on a regional basis. You can obtain further information by writing the United States Power Federation, P.O. Box 18485, Pensacola, Florida 32523.

The sport of power lifting tests an individual's raw strength. The lifts are slow and controlled, as opposed to the Olympic lifts, which require a combination of strength, speed, momentum and coordination. You will be performing some of the three power lifts when you perform the suggested routines in chapter 6. Power lifts can be performed in your normal lifting environments with the help of your training partner.

Squat. Place the bar across the back of your shoulders at the base of your neck. Space your hands evenly on the bar for balance. Your feet should be slightly wider than shoulder width apart. Lower yourself until your thighs are parallel to the floor, then return to standing position. Do not bounce, but move slowly and under control. Keep your back straight and your head up throughout the movement.

Photo 7-2

Photo 7-1

Bench Press. Lie on your bench (photo 7-3). Notice that your knees should be bent at right angles (90°) and your feet should be placed firmly on the ground. Your lower back and buttocks should be pressed down onto the bench throughout the entire movement. Grasp the bar where your hands feel most comfortable. This will probably be slightly wider than shoulder width. Lower the bar to your chest, pause, and then press it up until your arms straighten. Be careful to move slowly and under control. Do not bounce the bar off your chest, but rather pause for 2 full seconds before pressing the bar. **You should always use a spotter for this exercise.**

Photo 7-3   **Photo 7-4**

Dead Lift. Stand with your feet slightly more than shoulder width apart (photo 7-5). Bend at the knees so that your thighs are parallel with the ground. Keep your back as straight as possible and keep your head up as you do when squatting. Grasp the bar so that your arms are resting against the outside of your knees. Use a mixed grip, placing one hand on the bar with your palm toward you and the other palm facing away. A grip such as this will allow you to lift more weight and maintain greater control of the bar than a traditional grip.

When you are ready to lift, lean back slightly and initiate your pull by using the large muscles of the thighs, hips and buttocks. Do not use your back or arms, but rather keep your back and arms straight throughout the entire movement. The bar should start out touching your shins and remain in contact with your legs throughout the movement. As you near the completion of this exercise, use your upper back and shoulder muscles to help you stand up (photo 7-6).

Be sure to keep your head up throughout the movement, as this will help to keep your back straight, lessening the strain on your lower back.

Photo 7-5

Photo 7-6

Olympic Lifting

Olympic lifting contests consist of two lifts: the snatch and the clean and jerk. In the United States, the United States Weight Lifting Federation (USWLF) oversees Olympic lifting competitions. Meets are held on a regional basis and include participants 12 years of age and older.

Further information may be obtained by writing to the United States Weight Lifting Federation, 1750 East Boulder Street, Colorado Springs, CO 80909. The Amateur Athletic Union (AAU) of the United States also encourages youth lifting through its AAU/USA Junior Olympics program in weight lifting. For further information write to AAU House, 3400 West 86th Street, Indianapolis, IN 46268.

Olympic lifting requires strength as well as a tremendous amount of skill. Coordination, quickness, speed and balance all play important roles in a lifter's success. The Olympic lifts should be practiced with a broomstick or empty barbell bar to develop proper technique before attempting to perform them with actual weights.

You might try familiarizing yourself with these techniques by using them as part of your warm-up routine before daily lifting sessions. Your strength and flexibility should be developed for several months before you attempt to perform lifts with weights. If you decide to seriously try the sport of Olympic lifting, contact the USWLF to find the nearest training site that can give you quality guidance and coaching. This will be essential if you are to train safely and make progress.

Snatch. To perform the snatch correctly, you must bring the barbell from the floor to an overhead position (arms straight) in one continuous motion. In the starting position (photos 7-7A and 7-7B) notice that your feet should be slightly more than shoulder width apart, toes pointed forward and balance evenly distributed. With the bar resting against your shins, place your hands as far apart as possible while still being able to control the bar. It will require some practice to determine the hand spacing best for you. Your arms should be straight, thighs parallel with the ground, back flat and head up.

Photo 7-7A

Photo 7-7B

When you are ready to initiate your lift, lean back slightly and start your pull using the muscles of your thighs, hips and buttocks. This will set the bar in motion. You can add to this momentum by continuing the pull with the muscles in your upper back. Let your arms bend slightly so that your elbows ride up high. If this phase is well coordinated and your initial pull is powerful, the bar should ride up to about head level.

When the bar has reached its full height you should duck under it, straightening your arms and controlling the bar (photos 7-8A and 7-8B). The bar should actually travel in a straight line from the floor to this position. Be sure to keep the bar close to your body throughout the entire movement.

Photo 7-8A   **Photo 7-8B**

The final phase of this exercise (photos 7-9A and 7-9B) requires that you stand up, keeping your body still (no foot movement) with arms straight for 2 seconds. This third and final phase relies heavily on the strength in your thighs, hips and buttocks.

Photo 7-9A

Photo 7-9B

Clean and Jerk. The starting position for the clean and jerk is similar to the position for the dead lift. The major difference is that in the clean and jerk you should use the standard overhand grip. Keep your feet spread slightly wider than shoulder width apart, arms straight and resting against the outside of your knees; your thighs should be parallel to the ground; back flat and head up.

Start your pull using your thighs, hips and buttocks. Keep the bar against your shins when starting and think of pulling in a straight line. If you lean back slightly when initiating your pull this will help to position you correctly. As the bar rises off the ground elevate the muscles in your upper back. Bend your elbows upward and outward using your biceps to further pull the bar. Duck under the bar and catch it on your collarbone (photos 7-11A and 7-11B). Be careful not to let your elbows rest on your knees. This is illegal and will disqualify a lift in competition.

From this position rise to a standing position (photos 7-12A and 7-12B). This requires the muscles of your thighs, hips and buttocks to contract, driving your body upward. Pause in this standing position for a second and be sure you have your balance and a good grip on the bar. Bend your legs slightly and thrust the bar up over your head until your arms straighten. Although you may press the bar to some degree by using your arms, the majority of the bar's momentum should come from the driving force created by your thighs, hips and buttocks. As the bar rises up step forward with one leg (photos 7-13A and 7-13B) to lower your body under the bar. This requires both balance and timing, as you will find out quickly when you try it.

The final phase of this lift requires that you bring your body to a standing position, with the bar supported at arm's length overhead.

Photo 7-10A

Photo 7-10B

Photo 7-11A

Photo 7-11B

Photo 7-12A

Photo 7-12B

Photo 7-13A

Photo 7-13B

Photo 7-14A

Photo 7-14B

Some Final Thoughts

As an adolescent keep in mind that your bones are still growing and forming. Your tendons, ligaments and muscles also are in the growth stage. Any consistently repeated stress to these growing body parts may cause stress fractures or an actual wearing away of bones and underlying tissue. Overuse syndromes are very common to people your age.

Once you have such a syndrome, the treatment can range from complete rest to surgery, depending upon the severity and location of the injury. If severe enough, these injuries may even cause permanent damage.

Therefore, it is important to build a good muscular base and develop flexibility before attempting either heavy power lifts or Olympic lifts. You should train initially by following the routines that I have outlined in chapter 6. These routines will take you approximately one year to complete. During that time practice your Olympic lifting techniques using either a broomstick or a barbell bar. At the end of one year you should notice substantial strength increases and feel much more confident about your ability to lift weights.

If at that time you desire to lift competitively, contact the appropriate local organization to find a quality program with whom you can train and have fun.

VIII. Eating For Strength: A Nutritional Plan

As humans, we constantly are requiring our bodies to produce energy. We want to sit up, stand, walk, run faster, etc.; all of which require energy. As athletes, the demands we make are quite strenuous at times. The basis, then, for optimal physical performance starts with a sound nutritional plan, since we derive our energy from food.

Food is the fuel we use (1) to maintain and grow tissue, (2) to regulate the chemical and metabolic reactions constantly taking place in our bodies, and (3) to get the energy we need to successfully carry out tasks or to perform well in activity.

Poor nutritional practices will take their toll on the athlete and the nonathlete as well, resulting in reduced stamina and strength. Eating "healthy" can be rather simple however, and goes a long way in promoting optimal health and performance. Sound nutritional habits should be the basis of any conditioning program, strength training included. In this chapter we will examine what foods are, how our body uses them during physical activity, and how to safely and effectively maintain or alter weight.

Foods and Nutrients

Breaking foods down into nutrients is a common method of classifying and describing foods for their energy potential. There are six nutrients, and many foods are comprised of a combination of them. This next section will help you to understand each nutrient better.

WATER

Water is the most important of all nutrients in that it is needed by your body in uninterrupted supplies. It helps your body transport other nutrients and remove cellular waste products. It also plays a critical role in temperature regulation.

The need for water becomes greatest during physical activity and during hot and humid weather. It is important that you drink plenty of water, since your body cannot produce it as it can some other nutrients. In fact, you should drink water whenever you are thirsty, particularly during an exercise or athletic activity, and force yourself to drink water as a preventative measure throughout the day even if you are not thirsty.

MINERALS

Minerals are generally divided into two groups; those found in the body in large quantities and those which you need in very small amounts (referred to as 'trace' minerals). Minerals aid in the buildup and breakdown of other nutrients and are found in sufficient quantities with a normal, varied diet. Sodium, calcium, potassium, phosphorus, magnesium, sulfur and chlorides all are minerals which can be found in large quantities. There are at least fourteen known trace minerals. Iron, zinc, iodine and fluorides are perhaps the most important. Most of these can be derived from a varied diet, as shown later in this chapter.

Special mention should be made of iron, as it is the trace mineral found in greatest quantity in the body. Iron is particularly important for athletes and adolescents because it plays an important role in energy production, endurance and bone formation. Sometimes it is recommended that diets be supplemented with iron for individuals of your age group, but your family physician would be best able to guide you on a personal level in this matter.

Table 8-1 is a guide to sources and functions of the large minerals.

Table 8-1. Sources and functions of large minerals.

Mineral	Source	Function
Sodium	Salt, celery, beet greens and kale.	Maintains acid-base balance in cells and cellular pressures.
Calcium	Most dairy products including milk and eggs, green leafy vegetables and shellfish.	Bone and teeth formation, functioning of nerve tissue and blood clotting.
Potassium	Bananas, sweet potatoes, green vegetables and beets.	Plays an integral role in the contractility of muscle and affects level of excitation in nerve tissue.
Phosphorus	Milk, fish, eggs and poultry products.	Plays roles in the energy metabolism of muscles, metabolism of carbohydrates, fats and protein, nervous tissue metabolism, blood chemistry, skeletal growth, and transportation of fatty acids.
Magnesium	Beans, peas, rice, wheat, assorted nuts.	Along with calcium it maintains cellular balance in skeletal and cardiac muscle, nerve tissue and activates selected enzymes.
Sulfur	Amino acids in dietary proteins.	Component of cartilage and tendons.
Chlorine	Salt	Acid-base balances.
Iron*	Liver, lean meats, shellfish, soybeans, dried fruits, nuts, egg yolks and green leafy vegetables.	Formation of red blood cells, muscle growth and function, oxygen transport and tissue respiration.

*denotes trace mineral.

VITAMINS

Vitamins are small organic substances which function as chemical regulators. They play an important role in promoting growth and the maintenance of life, but contrary to popular belief *they provide no direct source of energy and they do not contribute significantly to body structure.* The vitamin needs of the athlete are actually about the same as the vitamin needs of a sedentary nonathlete.

Like minerals, vitamins can be grouped in two categories, based on how they are stored in the body. Vitamins A, D, E, and K are stored in the liver and in free fatty acids. They are referred to as fat-soluble vitamins. Vitamin C and the B-complex vitamins are stored in water, and the body needs to keep replenishing these vitamins on a more regular basis. The daily requirement of C can be met through such foods as vegetables and citrus fruits. The B-complex vitamins are found in many of the carbohydrate type foods which athletes commonly eat. As with minerals, a well-balanced meal plan using foods from the basic four food groups presented in table 8-4 should ensure an adequate supply of vitamins. Table 8-2 outlines sources and functions of both fat and water soluble vitamins.

Table 8-2. Sources and functions of vitamins.

FAT SOLUBLE VITAMINS

Vitamin	Source	Function
A	Liver, eggs, milk, dark green and dark yellow vegetables	Normal growth of bones, teeth and skin, normal vision
D	Fish, dairy products, eggs, and sunlight	Increases the retention and utilization of calcium and phosphorous, helps to ensure normal mineralization of bones
E	Vegetable oils, green leafy vegetables, nuts	Prevents unwanted oxidation of fatty acids and certain vitamins
K	Green leafy vegetables	Provides for the synthesis of prothrombin, used in blood clotting

Table 8-2. Sources and functions of vitamins (continued).

WATER SOLUBLE VITAMINS

Vitamin	Source	Function
Thiamine (B1)	Lean meat, grains, eggs, green leafy vegetables, milk, nuts	Carbohydrate metabolism, nerve function, formation of Niacin
Riboflavin (B2)	Milk, eggs, fish, meats, green leafy vegetables, whole grain foods	Energy metabolism
Niacin	Fish, poultry, meats, whole grain cereals, peanuts, dried beans and peas	Key role in the utilization of all nutrients, promotes growth, energy metabolism
B6	Meats, whole grain cereals, vegetables, bananas, and fish	Cellular function, production of short term energy, and protein metabolism
B12	Fish, milk and foods of animal origin	Central nervous system function, formation of blood, energy metabolism and promotion of growth
Ascorbic Acid (C)	Citrus fruits and juices, tomatoes, potatoes, cabbage and broccoli	Metabolism of other vitamins and amino acids, formation of supporting tissues (collagenous and fibrous), supporting tissue of capillary walls

CARBOHYDRATES

The most efficient sources of energy are the sugars and starches found in plants. These sugars and starches are referred to as carbohydrates. Fats and proteins also supply energy, but fats, which are a more concentrated form of energy, are generally stored. They are more effective as a long term energy source due to the complicated and lengthy process involved in their breakdown and ultimate use for energy. Proteins are a poor source of energy and are the last nutrient to supply energy, doing so in small amounts.

The process of digesting carbohydrates yields simple sugars which are absorbed from the intestinal tract and transported by the bloodstream to the liver. Here they are converted to glucose which

can be readily used for energy. A small amount of glucose is converted to 'glycogen,' whose importance will be discussed later in
this chapter. A large portion of the glucose then enters back into the
bloodstream and is transported to such body tissues as the brain
and muscles, kidneys, heart and other vital organs which need constant nourishment.

This constant need for glucose has dietary implications, since
only a relatively small amount of glucose can be stored in the body.
To keep glucose stores adequately filled it is important to eat balanced meals over the course of the day and possibly supplement
meals with carbohydrate snacks throughout the day, particularly if
you are an athlete who demands high energy output from your
body. Feelings of weakness, hunger, dizziness and even nausea
are common signs that your glucose stores are low. Low glucose
hinders reflexes and awareness, not only reducing your efficiency
on the athletic field but also making you less productive in the
classroom. The eating plan provided in this chapter will help you to
optimally develop and utilize your energy capabilities.

FATS

Fats should be an essential part of your diet. The amount which
you need, however, is constantly being studied and revised. There
seems to be a strong relationship between fats and the development of coronary heart disease, which often starts at a very early
age. Fats represent the most concentrated source of energy, con-
taining twice as much energy per gram as either carbohydrates or
protein. They are therefore well suited for storage and provide your
main source of energy during low-level, rhythmical activities which
are performed over long periods of time (15–60 minutes).

Fats are found in foods we like for flavor, such as creams, butter,
other dairy products, and red meat. As a result, fats can be quite
tempting, and are easily accessible. The American Heart
Association and most nutrition experts agree, however, that the
majority of your diet should come from complex carbohydrates, and
the eating plan presented in later pages will ensure that for you.

PROTEIN

Protein, the last of the six nutrients, is essential to your health
and well-being. However, the value of protein and the concern for it
are often exaggerated. Protein's most important contribution is for
tissue growth and repair. As an energy source it is poor, and only
contributes in small amounts when the more efficient nutrients of
fats and carbohydrates are unavailable.

Most of us eat more protein than we really need, and since our bodies store very little of it, the excess is excreted. In this process, the body loses water as well as protein, with a negative effect on the athlete in endurance events, particularly in warm weather. Diets high in protein are used for weight loss, often with severe, even life-threatening side effects, and you would be best advised to eat approximately 15% protein in your overall diet. A balanced and varied diet will ensure an adequate amount of high quality protein, whether you are a sedentary individual or an athlete.

Table 8-3 compares the sources and functions of carbohydrates, fats and proteins.

Table 8-3. Sources and functions of some principle nutrients.

Nutrient	Source	Function
Carbohydrate	Cereal and grain products, pastas, starchy vegetables, sugar and honey, and dried fruits	Efficient short-term energy source and metabolic primer for aerobic activity
Fat	Oils, butter, red and other meats with lard; mayonnaise and creamy salad dressings, nuts, and chocolate	Concentrated source of energy which is easily stored, primary energy source during aerobic activities; flavor and transports fat-soluble vitamins: A, D, E and K
Protein	Meat, fish, nuts, cereals and dairy products including eggs	Tissue repair and maintenance, synthesis of antibodies, enzymes and hormones; serves as a minor contributor to energy in exhaustive work

Nutrition: Implications for Athletic Performance

The basis for optimal performance is having the best blend of fuel possible to power your body. A well-balanced diet will provide this for you. Earlier in this chapter I referred to the basic four-food-group plan, which is a basic balanced dietary plan. It is a relatively simple plan, which has been around for years in concept. With some modifications it remains a sound guide for planning food intake.

The four-food-group plan is presented in table 8-4. Eating from this recommended serving schedule will ensure an adequate balance of all six nutrients. The recommendations of the U.S. Dietary

Guidelines suggest a diet which consists of 30% fat, with 10% coming from saturated sources, 10% from polyunsaturated, and the remaining 10% from monounsaturated; 55% carbohydrates, of which only 10% should be simple sugars and the remaining 45% complex; and 15% proteins. You can alter the amount of food you eat based on your energy needs.

Table 8-4. The four-food-group plan.

Food Category	Examples	Recommended Daily Servings
1. Milk and dairy products*	Mllk, cheese, ice creams, sour cream, yogurt, etc.	2
2. Meat and high protein foods**	Meat, fish, poultry, eggs, dried beans, peas, nuts, peanut butter, etc.	2
3. Vegetables and fruits	Green and yellow vegetables, citrus fruits, tomatoes, etc.	4
4. Cereals and grains	Enriched breads, cereals, flour, baked goods, whole grain products	4

*If you are consuming large quantities of milk or milk products, try substituting skim milk, nonfat milk or 2% milk. This measure will help to reduce the quantity of saturated fats in your diet.

**Fish, chicken, and high-protein vegetables contain significantly less saturated fats than many of the other protein sources common in diets.

PERFORMANCE DIETS

While a basic diet will provide adequate energy stores for a variety of athletic events, an understanding of energy systems will help you to understand how foods are used and where your energy is coming from.

Your body never uses only one type of system to provide energy, but rather receives energy from a blending of several systems. For some activities, one system will dominate over the other, making more of an energy contribution.

In activities of high intensity and short duration, like sprinting, you will receive most of your energy from your *anaerobic* system. Anaerobic refers to energy production without the use of oxygen; energy is derived from the stored glucose mentioned earlier. This system provides energy for activities lasting 10 seconds or less. In activities which range from 10 seconds to 2–3 minutes, glycogen, stored in the muscles and liver, contributes energy after the glucose stores start to deplete.

As the time involved in an activity progresses, the role of the anaerobic system starts to diminish and the *aerobic* system, or oxygen system, starts to play a greater role in supplying energy. Aerobic activity utilizes stored fat as its primary energy source, although glucose and glycogen are still used to 'prime the system'. Fats, as was mentioned earlier, are an efficient source of energy. Per unit of weight, they have twice the energy of carbohydrates and protein. The foods you eat, whether carbohydrates or fats, will be converted to and stored as fat after your glucose and glycogen stores are filled.

Athletes performing aerobic activities, like distance running, are usually thin since they keep using up their fat stores for energy. Aerobic activity also is used by individuals who wish to lose weight. Strength training, on the other hand, is an anaerobic activity, as an average set will only take approximately 30 seconds to complete. Such activity promotes muscular strength but does little to promote weight loss. General aerobic conditioning activities such as jogging, swimming, or aerobic dancing used in combination with strength training will help your overall athletic performance in a variety of sports, maintain your overall health and help you to look your best too. A balanced diet and exercise plan go hand in hand for promoting peak performance.

Energy Balance: Weight Loss, Gain and Maintenance

Weight control is of concern to most people, no matter what their age—athletes and nonathletes alike. For the young athlete who is constantly growing, it can be a troublesome concern, particularly in sports which have weight classifications.

Remember that as a teenager you are naturally growing larger and stronger. In addition, you are promoting the growth of muscle by strength training; this increase in muscle mass also will increase your body weight. It is perhaps more important to focus on your percentage of body fat, as mentioned in chapter 4, than on body weight. If you try to maintain a percentage of body fat that is optimal for athletic performance and health, you will not need to worry about increases in weight, as long as the increases are in lean body weight or the natural growth of bones and muscle.

The foods you eat and activities you participate in will influence changes in your body weight as well as changes in your body composition. The energy costs of foodstuffs and physical tasks are measured in units called calories. The more calories a food source has, the more potential energy it has. Likewise, the more physically demanding an activity is, the more calories you will have to expend to perform it.

In order to alter or maintain weight you need to change the caloric balance in your diet either toward a positive imbalance for weight gain, a negative imbalance for weight loss, or a balance of caloric intake and expenditure for weight maintenance. Figure 8-1 will help to illustrate this concept clearly.

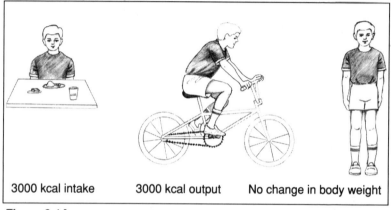

| 3000 kcal intake | 3000 kcal output | No change in body weight |

Figure 8-1A

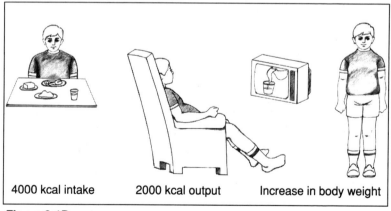

| 4000 kcal intake | 2000 kcal output | Increase in body weight |

Figure 8-1B

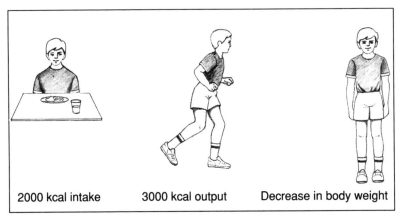

| 2000 kcal intake | 3000 kcal output | Decrease in body weight |

Figure 8-1C

Your daily energy needs can be calculated according to your height, weight, age and sex, as well as the amount of physical activity you participate in each day. These calculations are rather lengthy and involved for an individual of your age, however; they are much too difficult to present in a book such as this.

Your parents might find the program presented in Appendix B to be an easy and safe method of helping you to reach your weight goal, whether it be weight loss or gain, while eating nutritionally balanced meals.

Remember, an athlete's diet need not differ drastically from a nonathlete's. The major difference lies in how much you eat, based on energy needs, not in what you eat.

Diet is a critical consideration when you are trying to maximize your performance on either the athletic field or in the strength room. Using this chapter as a guide will point you in the right direction. If you want further information on either losing or gaining weight ask your physician, coach or parents for help.

IX. Sport-Specific Strength-Training Programs

This chapter is written for those who wish to strength train for a particular sport. Remember that no matter what sport you play it is important from a health perspective to maintain muscular balance in all the major muscle groups within your body. Training needs do vary from one sport to another however, and this chapter will help you to better target your needs.

If strength training is new for you, I suggest you follow the plans outlined in chapters 5 and 6 prior to using any of the training plans outlined in this chapter. This will help you become more familiar with strength-training concepts, exercises and techniques. It also will help you to build a base upon which to expand.

The principles and procedures outlined in chapters 5 and 6 should be applied when using these more specific programs unless you are otherwise directed. Be sure to start each exercise session with an appropriate warm-up and stretching phase.

Be patient and believe in the system. Proper training technique and form is important for achieving success and preventing injury. In time, your strength will increase and your sport skills should improve. Continue to work on your various skills, as strength training will enhance them but is not meant to substitute for them.

To locate a precise description and photo for each exercise in the lists in this chapter, refer to the numbers in the right-hand columns. Opposite *Leg Press,* for example, you will find *6-1 through 6-4.* The first number of each pair is the chapter number and the second number is the photo number.

Baseball and Softball

These sports require explosive muscular power for hitting, throwing and short bouts of sprinting. Flexibility is also important to maximize the body mechanics required for performing the skills specific to this sport and for preventing injury. Areas of particular importance include the legs, mid-torso region (particularly rotation) and the shoulder girdle.

During the off-season, follow the plan outlined below, training three times per week. During the season you can retain your strength levels by training once every five days.

Exercise	Chapter-Photo
Leg press/squat	6-1 through 6-4
Leg flexion	6-5 through 6-7
Leg extension	6-8 through 6-10
Heel raises	6-11 through 6-13
Lat pulldown	6-28 and 6-29
Incline press	6-16 and 6-17
Pull-over	6-18 and 6-19
Flies	6-20 and 6-21
Lateral raises	6-45 through 6-49
Dips	6-22 and 6-23
Bicep curls	6-56 through 6-63
Tricep extension	6-50 through 6-53
Wrist curls	6-65 and 6-66
Reverse wrist curls	same
Abdominal/low back (including rotation movements)	5-20 through 5-28

Basketball

Basketball requires both explosive muscular power and muscular endurance. The muscles of the legs and hips are critical for jumping performance. The muscles of the back will play a major role in pulling rebounds and loose balls into the body to gain possession. The muscles of the shoulders will offer support for shooting and maintaining a good defensive stance.

Train at the off-season and pre-season programs three times per week.

OFF-SEASON

Exercise	Chapter-Photo
Leg press/squat	6-1 through 6-4
Leg flexion	6-5 through 6-7
Heel raises	6-11 through 6-13
Pull-over	6-18 and 6-19
Bench press	6-14 and 6-15
Rowing	6-24 through 6-27
Overhead press	6-39 through 6-44
Upright rowing	6-35 and 6-36
Tricep extension	6-50 through 6-53
Bicep Curls	6-56 through 6-63
Abdominal/low back	5-20 through 5-28

PRE-SEASON

Exercise	Chapter-Photo
Leg press/squat	6-1 through 6-4
Leg flexion	6-5 through 6-7
Leg extension	6-8 through 6-10
Heel raises	6-11 through 6-13
Lat pulldown	6-28 and 6-29
Incline press	6-16 and 6-17
Lateral raises	6-45 through 6-49
Abdominal/low back	5-20 through 5-28

IN-SEASON

Train twice per week using (a) exercises on one day and (b) exercises the next.

Exercise		Chapter-Photo
Leg extension	(a)	6-8 through 6-10
Leg press/squat	(b)	6-1 through 6-4
Leg flexion	(a and b)	6-5 through 6-7
Pull-over	(a)	6-18 and 6-19
Lat pulldown	(b)	6-28 and 6-29
Bench press	(a)	6-14 and 6-15
Incline press	(b)	6-16 and 6-17
Lateral raises	(a)	6-45 through 6-49
Overhead press	(b)	6-39 through 6-44
Abdominal/low back		5-20 through 5-28

Football

Football requires speed, explosive power, and pushing strength. Due to the amount of contact involved, it also requires muscular integrity around the joints to prevent injury.

The off-season program should therefore focus on general conditioning and strength gain. Training three times per week will help you achieve these goals. During the season, when practice sessions, strategy sessions and games demand your time, strive to maintain your strength by training twice per week.

Exercise	Chapter-Photo

*All players, regardless of position, should perform leg exercises at the beginning of the workout session prior to using the position- specific upper-body exercises.

Leg press/squat	6-1 through 6-4
Leg flexion	6-5 through 6-7
Heel raises	6-11 through 6-13

(Offensive and defensive line)

Close grip bench press	6-54 and 6-55
Incline dumbbell press	6-16 and 6-17
Overhead press	6-39 through 6-44
Tricep extension	6-50 through 6-53
Dips	6-22 and 6-23
Rowing	6-24 through 6-27
Bicep curls	6-56 through 6-63
Abdominal/low back	5-20 through 5-28

(Linebackers and tight ends)

Close grip bench press	6-54 and 6-55
Incline dumbbell press	6-16 and 6-17
Tricep extension	6-50 through 6-53
Lateral raises	6-45 through 6-49
Overhead press	6-39 through 6-44
Pull-over	6-18 and 6-19
Bicep curls	6-56 through 6-63
Abdominal/low back	5-20 through 5-28

(Wide receivers, secondary and quarterbacks)

Incline press	6-16 and 6-17
Overhead press	6-39 through 6-44
Lat pulldown	6-28 and 6-29
Bicep curls (dumbbells)	6-60 through 6-63
Tricep extension	6-50 through 6-53
Lateral raises	6-45 through 6-49
Abdominal/low back	5-20 through 5-28

Gymnastics

Gymnastics requires a unique blend of muscular strength and endurance for such events as the rings, horizontal or uneven bars, and floor exercises. Some events, such as the balance beam and vaulting, require more muscular power than some of the floor exercise moves.

A general conditioning program, performed three times per week, will enhance joint integrity and strengthen all of the major muscle groups. Muscular strength and endurance also will be developed by your training for specific movement skills.

Exercise	Chapter-Photo
Leg press/squat	6-1 through 6-4
Leg flexion	6-5 through 6-7
Heel raises	6-11 through 6-13
Incline press	6-16 and 6-17
Pull-over	6-18 and 6-19
Flies	6-20 and 6-21
Lat pulldown	6-28 and 6-29
Dips	6-22 and 6-23
Pull-ups	6-30 through 6-32
Overhead press	6-39 through 6-44
Shoulder shrugs	6-33 and 6-34
Lateral raises	6-45 through 6-49
Upright rowing	6-35 and 6-36
Abdominal/low back	5-20 through 5-28

Hockey

Hockey requires short, fast bursts of speed and agility. The muscles most responsible for muscular power in these types of movements are the hips and legs. The wrists and forearms also are important in the skills of shooting and passing.

Off-season training should be conducted three days per week. During the season, the number of training days per week can be reduced to once every five days to retain the strength levels produced in the off-season.

Exercise	Chapter-Photo
Leg press/squat	6-1 through 6-4
Leg flexion	6-5 through 6-7
Leg extension	6-8 through 6-10
Heel raises	6-11 through 6-13
Rowing	6-24 through 6-27
Bench press	6-14 and 6-15
Upright rowing	6-35 and 6-36
Lateral raises	6-45 through 6-49
Wrist curls	6-65 and 6-66
Reverse wrist curls	same
Abdominal/low back (including rotation movements)	5-20 through 5-28

Lacrosse

Lacrosse is similar to hockey with respect to lower body demands, but the shoulder involvement is slightly different since the stick is held above the waist and the ball is moved with a throwing-type movement.

Train three days per week during the off-season to improve your strength. During the season, reduce your training to once every five days.

Exercise	Chapter-Photo
Leg flexion	6-5 through 6-7
Leg extension	6-8 through 6-10
Heel raises	6-11 through 6-13
Pull-over	6-18 and 6-19
Bench press	6-14 and 6-15
Overhead press	6-39 through 6-44
Bicep curls	6-56 through 6-63
Tricep extension	6-50 through 6-53
Wrist curls	6-65 and 6-66
Reverse wrist curls	same
Abdominal/low back (including rotation movements)	5-20 through 5-28

Racquet Sports

Racquet sports involve most of the major muscle groups in the body. The power for a stroke starts with the legs and the hips. The rotation of the mid-torso region assures a smooth transition of power from the legs to the upper body. The arms and wrists finish the movement. A well-balanced training program which promotes both power and muscular endurance is presented.

Many racquet sport seasons are now extending into year-round commitments. Your coach can best guide you as to how often you should strength-train based on each season.

Exercise	Chapter-Photo
Leg flexion	6-5 through 6-7
Leg extension	6-8 through 6-10
Heel raises	6-11 through 6-13
Pull-over	6-18 and 6-19
Flies	6-20 and 6-21
Rowing	6-24 through 6-27
Lateral raises	6-45 through 6-49
Bicep curls	6-56 through 6-63
Tricep extension	6-50 through 6-53
Wrist curls	6-65 and 6-66
Reverse wrist curls	same
Abdominal/low back	5-20 through 5-28

(inlcuding rotation movements)

Soccer

Soccer requires power from the hip and leg muscles for running, jumping and kicking. Strength in the shoulder girdle will help with throw-ins and the muscles of the upper back and neck regions will come into play during plays involving the head.

To maximize your strength gains, train two to three times per week year round, depending upon your schedule.

Exercise	Chapter-Photo
Leg press/squat	6-1 through 6-4
Leg flexion	6-5 through 6-7
Leg extension	6-8 through 6-10
Heel raises	6-11 through 6-13
Pull-over	6-18 and 6-19
Incline press	6-16 and 6-17
Upright rowing	6-35 and 6-36
Lateral raises	6-45 through 6-49
Shoulder shrugs	6-33 and 6-34
Tricep extension	6-50 through 6-53
Abdominal/low back	5-20 through 5-28

Swimming

Swimming, unlike many other sports, necessitates strength in pulling movements as opposed to pushing movements. The focus should therefore be on pulling, although general muscular conditioning is important for the recovery phase of many strokes and for creating muscular balance and symmetry around the skeletal structure of the body.

Like the racquet sports, swimming is often a year-round commitment. Your coach can best guide you as to how often to train based on changes in seasonal goals.

Exercise	Chapter-Photo
Leg extension	6-8 through 6-10
Leg flexion	6-5 through 6-7
Heel raises	6-11 through 6-13
Pull-over	6-18 and 6-19

Exercise	Chapter-Photo
Flies	6-20 and 6-21
Lat pulldown	6-28 and 6-29
Incline press	6-16 and 6-17
Pull-ups	6-30 through 6-32
Dips	6-22 and 6-23
Upright rowing	6-35 and 6-36
Tricep extension	6-50 through 6-53
Bicep curls	6-56 through 6-63
Abdominal/low back	5-20 through 5-28

Track and Field

The sport of track and field involves a number of diverse skills. Training will therefore vary, depending upon the event an athlete finds himself participating in. Strength-training plans are presented by category to help you tailor a program to your specific needs.

Strength-training should take place three days per week.

MIDDLE DISTANCE AND DISTANCE RUNNERS

Exercise	Chapter-Photo
Leg press/squat	6-1 through 6-4
Leg flexion	6-5 through 6-7
Leg extension	6-8 through 6-10
Heel raises	6-11 through 6-13
Bench press	6-14 and 6-15
Lat pulldown	6-28 and 6-29
Overhead press	6-39 through 6-44
Upright rowing	6-35 and 6-36
Dips	6-22 and 6-23
Pull-ups	6-30 through 6-32
Tricep extension	6-50 through 6-53
Bicep curls	6-56 through 6-63
Abdominal/low back	5-20 through 5-28

SPRINTERS AND JUMPERS

Exercise	Chapter-Photo
Leg press/squat	6-1 through 6-4
Leg flexion	6-5 through 6-7
Leg extension	6-8 through 6-10
Heel raises	6-11 through 6-13
Bench press	6-14 and 6-15
Upright rowing	6-35 and 6-36
Incline press	6-16 and 6-17
Shoulder shrugs	6-33 and 6-34
Dips	6-22 and 6-23
Rowing	6-24 through 6-27
Abdominal/low back	5-20 through 5-28

WEIGHT AND THROW EVENTS

Exercises are designed to be used on alternate (a and b) days. Athletes should lift four times per week using each group of exercises twice.

Exercise		Chapter-Photo
Squat	(a)	6-1 and 6-2
Leg press	(b)	6-3 and 6-4
Leg flexion	(a and b)	6-5 through 6-7
Heel raises	(a and b)	6-11 through 6-13

(a day)

Pull-over	6-18 and 6-19
Rowing	6-24 through 6-27
Lat pulldown	6-28 and 6-29
Upright rowing	6-35 and 6-36
Shoulder shrugs	6-33 and 6-34
Bicep curls	6-56 through 6-63

(b day)

Bench press	6-14 and 6-15
Incline press	6-16 and 6-17
Overhead press (dumbbell)	6-39 through 6-44
Flies	6-20 and 6-21
Tricep extension	6-50 through 6-53
Abdominal/low back	5-20 through 5-28
(including rotation movements)	

Volleyball

Volleyball is a power sport which requires hip and leg strength for jumping competitively. Shoulder and arm strength will improve ball-handling skills. Timing and mechanics are just as important. A general strength program will enhance existing jumping and skill programs and should be performed three days per week year round.

Exercise	Chapter-Photo
Leg press/squat	6-1 through 6-4
Leg flexion	6-5 through 6-7
Heel raises	6-11 through 6-13
Incline press	6-16 and 6-17
Pull-over	6-18 and 6-19
Flies	6-20 and 6-21
Shoulder shrugs	6-33 and 6-34
Tricep extensions	6-50 through 6-53
Wrist curls	6-65 and 6-56
Abdominal/low back	5-20 through 5-28

Wrestling

Wrestling requires strength and endurance in virtually every muscle group throughout the body. The hips and legs play a major role in controlling takedowns, placing various holds on an opponent, and neutralizing an opponent's hold on you. Pulling muscles are used to keep an opponent in close, and pushing muscles are needed to break holds. The muscles of the neck also are important to the wrestler and need to be trained as well.

An off-season program is presented. It is designed to develop overall body strength training three days per week. During the season the focus should shift toward maintaining strength and enhancing endurance capabilities. The same or similar exercises may be performed, as in the off-season but the frequency of training may be reduced to twice per week, supplementing your normal training sessions.

Exercise	Chapter-Photo
Leg flexion	6-5 through 6-7
Heel raises	6-11 through 6-13
Rowing	6-24 through 6-27
Incline press	6-16 and 6-17
Upright rowing	6-35 and 6-36
Flies	6-20 and 6-21
Shoulder shrugs	6-33 and 6-34
Lateral raises	6-45 through 6-49
Pull-ups	6-30 through 6-32
Dips	6-22 and 6-23
Bicep curls	6-56 through 6-63
Abdominal/low back	5-20 through 5-28

If your sport is not among those listed in this chapter, you can design your own program using these programs as a guide. First, analyze which muscles are most required by the skills involved in your sport. Then develop a program accordingly, applying the principles presented in this book. Keep in mind that ideally all of your major muscle groups should be strengthened to help you prevent injuries. You may wish to include an extra exercise or two for those muscles which play an important role in your sport.

Appendix A
Recording Forms

Form 4-1. Recording form for fitness assessment scores.

Assessment/ Fitness Level	Pull-ups/ Flexed Arm Hand	Sit-ups	Long Jump	Sit- and- Reach	Body Composition
EXCELLENT					
GOOD					
AVERAGE					
BELOW AVG.					
LOW					

Equation 4-1. Calculation of ideal body weight based on percent body fat and present weight.

[Total Body Weight x Percent Fat] /100 = Fat Weight

[_____ x _____] /100 = _____

[(150)   x   (20)   ] /100 =   (30 lbs.)

[Total Body Weight - Fat Weight] /   = Lean Body Weight

[_____ - _____] /   = _____

[(150)   -   (30)   ] /   =   (120 lbs.)

[Lean Body Weight x 100] / [Ideal Percent Lean Body Weight] =

[(120) x 100] / [(90)] =

[12000] / [90] =

133.33 lbs. (Ideal Body Weight @ 10% Fat)

Ideal lean body weight percentages can be found by sport in table 4-7.

Form 5-1. Daily Workout Recorder.

NAME _____

DATE												
EXERCISES	REPS	REPS	REPS	REPS	REPS	REPS	REPS	REPS	REPS	REPS	REPS	REPS

Table 6-1. Daily Workout Recorder.

NAME _____

DATE												
EXERCISES	WT / REPS	WT / REPS	WT / REPS	WT / REPS	WT / REPS	WT / REPS	WT / REPS	WT / REPS	WT / REPS	WT / REPS	WT / REPS	WT / REPS

Appendix B

Dear Parents:

Nutrition is an important issue in the overall health of your child, whether or not they are an athlete. Some of you may wish to help your child safely lose or gain weight. The principles presented in chapter 8 will provide a starting point for discussions on nutrition but may not be a specific enough guide for your child's needs.

The PERSONALIZED NUTRITION AND EXERCISE PLAN(c) is a computerized meal and exercise plan designed to help your child either gain, lose or maintain weight, depending upon their goals. Personalized menus are written for your child based on the foods they like to eat. The meal plans are easy to prepare and follow current U.S. Dietary Guidelines for carbohydrate, fat, protein, vitamin and mineral consumption. The focus of the 18 – 20 page packet is educational and contains a wealth of information on eating and nutrition, providing you and your child with an opportunity to discuss better nutrition together in a directed, easy to understand format.

To order the PERSONALIZED NUTRITION AND EXERCISE PLAN(c) simply:

1) Complete the *Personalized Nutrition and Exercise Plan* questionnaire (photocopied forms are acceptable).

2) Mail the completed questionnaire with a check or money order for $19.50 made payable to:

    SMITH PERSONAL FITNESS AGENCY, LTD.
    P.O. Box 922
    East Hampton, NY 11937

Hopefully, this plan will serve as an extension to *Youth Strength Training*, providing you and your child another educational opportunity through which you can interact.

PERSONALIZED NUTRITION AND EXERCISE PLAN

SECTION I. DEMOGRAPHIC DATA

Please print with a ballpoint pen.

Name _____
                        (First)   (Last)

Address_____
                (Street Number and Name)   (Apt. #)

_____   _____   _____
            (City)   (State)   (Zip)

Age: _____   Sex: Male ☐   Female ☐

Height: _____   _____   _____
            (Feet)   (Inches)   (Fraction)

Current Weight: _____

Desired Weight: _____

SECTION II. PHYSICAL ACTIVITY SPECTRUM

Physical activity at work (choose nearest whole number):

(1 = sedentary desk job; 5 = construction)

```
  |         |         |         |         |
  1         2         3         4         5
```

Leisure time activity (choose nearest whole number):

(1 = weekend golf; 5 = 3 mile runs / 4 days / week)

```
  |         |         |         |         |
  1         2         3         4         5
```

SECTION III. MENU OPTIONS

From the food categories below, select the foods you would like to have included in your menus. For categories 1 – 18 you must select at least one food from each category otherwise we will select one for you.

With an increased number of selections your menus will show greater variety. Categories 19 – 20 are optional and you need not make selections unless you wish to.

Category 1
A ☐milk, skim   **B** ☐milk, non-fat   **C** ☐milk, 2%

Category 2
A ☐yogurt, skim milk   **C** ☐yogurt, fruit   **E** ☐choc. milk, non-fat
B ☐yogurt, regular milk   **D** ☐whole milk   **F** ☐cottage cheese

Category 3
A ☐egg   **C** ☐ricotta cheese   **E** ☐american cheese
B ☐mozzarella   **D** ☐cheddar cheese   **F** ☐swiss cheese
                                                              G ☐canadian bacon

Category 4
A ☐chicken   **C** ☐hot dog   **E** ☐tuna
B ☐turkey   **D** ☐corned beef   **F** ☐crab, canned
                                                              G ☐peanut butter

Category 5
A ☐chuck steak   **D** ☐round steak   **H** ☐lamb chops
B ☐flank steak   **E** ☐rump steak   **I** ☐lamb roast
C ☐tenderloin   **F** ☐sirloin   **J** ☐lamb shoulder
                              G ☐lamb leg

Category 6
A ☐cornish hen   **E** ☐ground beef   **I** ☐pork roast
B ☐fish, fresh & frzn.   **F** ☐ground round   **J** ☐veal cutlets
C ☐shrimp   **G** ☐pork/ham   **K** ☐veal chops
D ☐scallops   **H** ☐pork chops   **L** ☐veal roast

Category 7
A ☐avocado   **C** ☐almonds   **F** ☐walnuts
B ☐olives, green   **D** ☐pecans   **G** ☐cream cheese
C ☐shrimp   **E** ☐peanuts, dry roast   **H** ☐bacon, crisp

Category 8
A ☐diet margarine

Category 9

A ☐cream, light   **C** ☐1000 island dressing   **F** ☐sour cream
B ☐fresh dressing   **D** ☐italian dressing   **G** ☐blue cheese dressing
    E ☐mayonnaise   **H** ☐tartar sauce

Category 10

A ☐raisin bread   **D** ☐toast   **G** ☐puffed cereal
B ☐bagel   **E** ☐bran flakes, 40%   **H** ☐cooked cereal
C ☐english muffin   **F** ☐cereal, dry   **I** ☐cooked grits
    J ☐doughnut, plain

Category 11

A ☐bread, any kind   **C** ☐graham crackers   **E** ☐plain muffin
B ☐melba toast   **D** ☐soda crackers   **F** ☐cooked rice

Category 12

A ☐cooked spaghetti   **F** ☐corn, off cob   **L** ☐mashed potatoes
B ☐cooked noodles   **G** ☐corn, on cob   **M** ☐squash
C ☐cooked macaroni   **H** ☐lima beans   **N** ☐biscuit
D ☐beans, kidney   **I** ☐parsnips   **O** ☐corn bread
E ☐lentils, cooked   **J** ☐peas   **P** ☐corn muffins
    K ☐baked potatoes   **Q** ☐yam

Category 13

A ☐apple juice   **D** ☐grapefruit   **G** ☐pineapple juice
B ☐banana   **E** ☐grape juice   **H** ☐prunes
C ☐grapefruit juice   **F** ☐orange juice   **I** ☐apricot juice
    J ☐papaya

Category 14

A ☐apple   **F** ☐raspberries   **L** ☐orange
B ☐apricot   **G** ☐strawberries   **M** ☐peach
C ☐apricot, dried   **H** ☐cider, any kind   **N** ☐pear
D ☐blackberries   **I** ☐dates   **O** ☐plum
E ☐blueberries   **J** ☐mango   **P** ☐raisins

Category 15

A ☐apple sauce   **D** ☐cantaloupe   **G** ☐nectarine
B ☐cherries   **E** ☐honeydew   **H** ☐pineapple
C ☐grapes   **F** ☐watermelon   **I** ☐tangerine

Category 16

A ☐cucumber   **C** ☐tomato   **F** ☐green pepper
B ☐vegetable juice   **D** ☐tomato juice   **G** ☐celery
    E ☐carrots   **H** ☐cauliflower

Category 17

A ☐asparagus
B ☐bean sprouts

C ☐beets
D ☐broccoli

E ☐brussel sprouts
F ☐cabbage
G ☐eggplant

Category 18

A ☐collards
B ☐kale
C ☐mustard greens
D ☐spinach

E ☐turnip greens
F ☐mushrooms
G ☐okra
H ☐string beans

I ☐artichokes
J ☐rutabago
K ☐sauerkraut
L ☐turnips
M ☐zucchini

OPTIONAL CHOICES

Category 19

A ☐lettuce
B ☐radishes

C ☐chicory
D ☐endive

E ☐escarole
F ☐parsley
G ☐watercress

Category 20

A ☐cake, angel food
B ☐cake, fruit
C ☐cake, pound

D ☐cupcake, with icing
E ☐candy bar, choc.
F ☐chocolate fudge
G ☐marshmallows, reg.

H ☐choc. chip cookies
I ☐oatmeal cookies
J ☐sugar cookies
K ☐pudding

SECTION IV. EXERCISE OPTIONS

Please select the exercises you wish to enjoy.

(1) ☐ walk/jog

(3) ☐ row

(5) ☐ aerobic dance

(2) ☐ stationary cycle

(4) ☐ swim

Glossary

Aerobic — an energy system which uses fats and protein to create energy. You use this energy system when you play sports like basketball, aerobic dancing, distance running and other activities which require large amounts of oxygen for extended periods of time.

Anaerobic — an energy system which uses carbohydrates to power short-term activities like sprinting, a football play, wrestling or gymnastics.

Body Building — a form of weight-lifting competition in which participants are judged on size, shape, definition and symmetry in selected muscle groups. Weights are not lifted in competitions but subjects pose to show the judges their muscular development.

Carbohydrate — a nutrient which provides anaerobic energy when broken down. Carbohydrates are found in pasta, vegetables, fruits, cereals and grains.

Exercise — any specific movement which stimulates specific, selected muscles.

Fat — a nutrient which provides aerobic energy in its breakdown. Fats are found in beef, pork, dairy products, shellfish and vegetables.

Isokinetic — a type of strength training in which the speed of movement is constant and the resistance varies.

Isometric — a type of strength training in which you exert force against an immovable resistance (ie: pushing against a wall).

Isotonic — a type of strength training in which your muscles contract against a fixed resistance (ie: pull-ups, push-ups, lifting barbells and dumbbells).

K-cal — (kilocalorie) — the equivalent of 1 Calorie. Calories are used to measure and describe the potential energy content of foods. The higher a food's caloric value the more potential energy it has.

Lactic Acid — a by-product of anaerobic exercise and energy production which, in large enough quantities, can cause muscular discomfort.

LBW — lean body weight or that portion of your weight comprised of bone and muscle mass as opposed to fat tissue.

Olympic LIfting — a form of weight-lifting competition in which the participant gets three attempts at the snatch and the clean and jerk. The best score is taken for each lift and the two scores are added together for a total score.

Overload — requiring your muscles to work against resistances greater than they are normally accustomed to.

Power Lifting — a form of weight-lifting competition in which the participant gets three attempts at the squat, bench press and dead lift. The best score is taken for each lift and the three scores are added together for a total score.

Progression — a systematic program or schedule to **overload** your muscles.

Protein — a nutrient which is used primarily for tissue growth and repair but may provide some energy in aerobic activities. Protein is found in fish, meat, dairy products and vegetables.

Repetition — a performance of a particular **exercise** from start to finish.

Resistance — any weight, object or pressure used to create an **overload**.

Set — the grouping of several successive **repetitions** together.

Super Set — the grouping of several **sets** together.

Index